R. Albert Mohler, Jr.

Acts 1–12

The Church Is Born

GOOD BOOK GUIDE

8-Session Bible Study

I0807111

Acts 1-12 For You

These studies are adapted from *Acts 1–12 For You*. If you are reading *Acts 1–12 For You* alongside this Good Book Guide, here is how the studies in this booklet link to the chapters of *Acts 1–12 For You*:

Study One > Ch 1
Study Two > Ch 3-5
Study Three > Ch 5
Study Four > Ch 6
Study Five > Ch 7
Study Six > Ch 8
Study Seven > Ch 9-10
Study Eight > Ch 11

Find out more about *Acts 1–12 For You* at:
www.thegoodbook.com/for-you

Acts 1–12: The Church Is Born
A Good Book Guide

This edition printed 2025.

Published by The Good Book Company

thegoodbook COMPANY

thegoodbook.com | thegoodbook.co.uk
thegoodbook.com.au | thegoodbook.co.nz

A CIP catalogue record for this book is available from the British Library.

Design by André Parker and Drew McCall

ISBN: 9781802541533 | JOB-008393 | Printed in India

Contents

Introduction 4
Why Study Acts 1 – 12? 5

1. Promises 7
Acts 1:1-26

2. The Spirit-Fueled Church 13
Acts 2:1 – 4:4

3. Church Challenges 19
Acts 4:5 – 5:42

4. I See the Heavens Opened 25
Acts 6:1 – 7:60

5. Beyond Jerusalem 31
Acts 8:1-40

6. The Most Unlikely Conversion 37
Acts 9:1-43

7. To the Gentiles 43
Acts 10:1 – 11:30

8. The Apostle, the Angel, and the King 51
Acts 12:1-25

Leader's Guide 57

Introduction

One of the Bible writers described God's word as "a lamp for my feet, a light on my path" (Psalm 119:105, NIV). God gave us the Bible to tell us about who he is and what he wants for us. He speaks through it by his Spirit and lights our way through life.

That means that we need to look carefully at the Bible and uncover its meaning—but we also need to apply what we've discovered to our lives.

Good Book Guides are designed to help you do just that. The sessions in this book are interactive and easy to lead. They're perfect for use in groups or for personal study.

Let's take a look at what is included in each session.

Talkabout: Every session starts with an ice-breaker question, designed to get people talking around a subject that links to the Bible study.

Investigate: These questions help you explore what the passage is about.

Apply: These questions are designed to get you thinking practically: what does this Bible teaching mean for you and your church?

Explore More: These optional sections help you to go deeper or to explore another part of the Bible which connects with the main passage.

Getting Personal: These sections are a chance for personal reflection. Some groups may feel comfortable discussing these, but you may prefer to look at them quietly as individuals instead—or leave them out.

Pray: Here, you're invited to pray in the light of the truths and challenges you've seen in the study.

Each session is also designed to be easily split into two! Watch out for the **Apply** section that comes halfway through, and stop there if you haven't got time to do the whole thing in one go.

In the back of the book, you'll find a **Leader's Guide**, which provides helpful notes on every question, along with everything else that group leaders need in order to facilitate a great session and help the group uncover the riches of God's light-giving word.

Why Study Acts 1 - 12?

The story of Jesus does not end with the resurrection of Jesus or even with the ascension of Jesus.

This is why Luke decided (or, from the heavenly rather than human perspective, why Luke was inspired by God's Spirit) to write a second volume to follow his Gospel, to chronicle the events of the early church—what we call the book of Acts.

We might also call it "The Book of What Jesus Did Next." In Acts 1:1, Luke states that his first book was about all that Jesus "began to do and teach." The implication is that Acts is the record of what Jesus continued to do and to teach, by his Spirit, in his church.

The first twelve chapters of Acts include some of the most famous portions of Scripture: the ascension of Jesus; the coming of the Spirit at Pentecost; the first Christian martyrdom; the conversion of the church's arch-persecutor, Saul; and the coming of the gospel to the Gentiles. Behind each event the sovereign hand of God is at work, giving birth to his church, shaping his church, using his church, and growing his church.

We meet so many individuals in these chapters, but God is always the primary actor. He uses the most unlikely of people to spread the gospel, like the impetuous Peter or even the murderous Saul. But it is *his* work, through people. Acts reminds us that God is sovereign in our lives and in his world, even when we don't understand what he is doing. We can be confident that the Lord is building his church and pursuing the good of his people—and we can feel privileged that he calls us to join him in this work.

These eight studies will chart the birth of the church—a church that still stands, that we are members of by faith, and that has the same mission as the one started in Acts: a task unfinished, of being Christ's witnesses "to the end of the earth" (Acts 1:8).

Creation

Fall

Noah

Abraham

Joseph

Exodus from Egypt

Israel reaches promised land

King David

Kingdom divided (Judah/Israel)

Israel exiled

Judah exiled

Judah returns

Jesus Christ

Pentecost

Jerusalem destroyed

Revelation written

Now

Jesus' return
New creation

GOOD BOOK GUIDE — BIBLE TIMELINE —

Acts c. 30-44 AD

c. 30 Jesus ascends; Pentecost

c. 35 Paul converted

c. 44 Peter imprisoned; Herod Agrippa dies

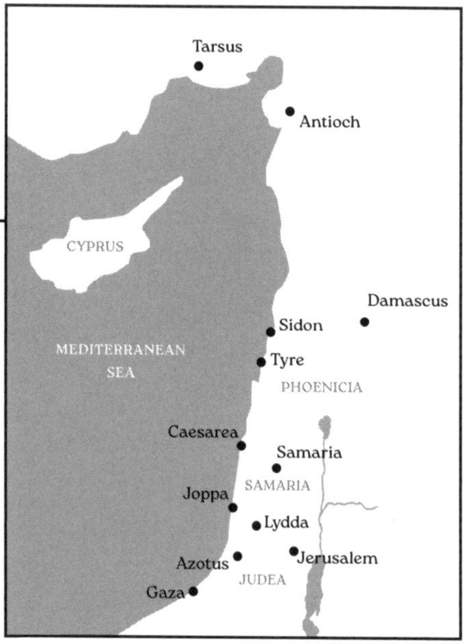

1

Promises

Acts 1:1-26

Talkabout

1. What is the hardest thing you have ever been asked to do?

- Did you back out or did you take it on? If the latter, were you successful, and why?

Investigate

Read Acts 1:1-11

DICTIONARY

Was taken up (v 2): ascended into heaven.

Apostles (v 2): the men chosen by Jesus to be witnesses to his resurrection and to teach with his authority.

John (v 5): John the Baptist. (See Luke 3:1-17.)

Restore the kingdom (v 6): bring about all God's Old Testament promises.

Jerusalem, Judea, and **Samaria** (v 8): see map on opposite page.

2. How does Luke describe what he recounted in "the first book"—the Gospel of Luke" (v 1-2)?

3. What did Jesus do after he had risen (v 3)?

4. What did Jesus tell his apostles...
   - they must do (v 4-5)?
   - they must be (v 8)?

5. Imagine you were one of those first followers, in a city that killed your King and hates your message. How would you have felt hearing verse 8?

6. After Jesus ascended back to heaven, what did the angels (the "two men ... in white robes") most want his followers to know (v 10-11)?

Explore More | OPTIONAL

Jesus' ascension into heaven is essential to the Christian faith.

- What do these passages teach us about the significance of the ascension?
  - Philippians 2:6-11
  - Ephesians 1:20-23
  - Hebrews 4:14-16; 7:23-25

Apply

7. What difference should it make to us to remember that "this Jesus … will come in the same way as [the apostles] saw him go" (v 11)?

8. What part do we have to play in the "Great Commission" of verse 8?

- What happens if we forget about the role of the Holy Spirit in this?

- What difference does it make if we know we have received his power?

Getting Personal | OPTIONAL

Do you tend to seek to obey Christ without relying on the Spirit's power, but rather on your own? Or do you tend to shrink back from witnessing about Christ because you feel powerless to do so?

How does verse 8 both encourage and challenge you? How do you need to change your attitude or your actions?

Investigate

📖 **Read Acts 1:12-26**

DICTIONARY

Peter and John... (v 13): this verse names all the original disciples, except Judas the betrayer.

With one accord (v 14): in unity with each other.

Lots (v 26): dice used to make decisions.

9. What did these Christians do while they waited for the Spirit (v 12-14)?

10. What do verses 15-26 teach us about...
    - what happened to Judas after he betrayed Jesus?
    - the Old Testament Scriptures?

- the qualifications for being an apostle?

Getting Personal | OPTIONAL

Judas' life and death is a sobering reminder to all of us of the need to genuinely examine ourselves to see if we are truly trusting in Christ.

None of us are above or beyond abandoning Christ. We must always be on guard against chasing after fleeting riches. Instead, we must walk each day in faith and repentance.

What things in your life most tempt you to betray Christ for the things of this world? How is knowing Christ better than those things?

What will obedience, and/or repentance, look like for you?

Apply

11. How do these verses encourage us to rely on the Old Testament Scripture and the apostles' teaching (that is, the New Testament)?

    - What would true reliance on their authority look like in our day-to-day lives?

12. How will you encourage each other to take on the hard but Spirit-enabled challenge of taking the gospel message "to the end of the earth"? What will that mean for each of you this week?

Pray

Thank God...

- *that Jesus is ascended and reigning.*
- *for the charge he gave to, and gives to, his church, to share the gospel throughout the earth.*
- *for the Spirit-given power to fulfill that commission.*

Ask God...

- *to show you your part in that commission, both as a church and as individuals.*
- *to help you rely on his Spirit as you seek to share Christ.*
- *to help you rely on the authority of the apostles in your daily lives (speak to God about any ways you need his help specifically to do this).*

2

The Spirit-Fueled Church

Acts 2:1 - 4:4

The Story So Far...

Jesus tasked his followers with taking the gospel to the end of the earth, before ascending into heaven. His people prayed as they waited for the Spirit.

Talkabout

1. What makes a good church? How would you answer that question in one or two sentences?

Investigate

Read Acts 2:1-14

DICTIONARY

Pentecost (v 1): festival celebrating the giving of God's law to Moses (see Exodus 19 – 40) and the wheat harvest.

Devout (v 5): committed; religious.

Proselytes (v 11): non-Jews who worshiped the God of Israel.

This event is one of the three most important moments in redemptive history. The first was creation, when God created the stage on which he would work out his sovereign plan. The second was the death and resurrection of the Lord Jesus. The third is Pentecost—the birth of the church.

2. Read Ezekiel 37:1-14 and Exodus 19:9, 16-25. How do these verses help us grasp the significance of the sound like wind and the tongues as of fire that demonstrated the coming of the Spirit?

3. Who did the event affect in…
   - Acts 2:1-4?
   - v 5-11?
   - How is the Spirit already working to fulfill Jesus' commission in 1:8?

4. In what different ways did people there respond to what they had seen and heard (v 11-13)?

📖 **Read Acts 2:14-47**

DICTIONARY

Prophesy (v 17, 18): proclaim truths about God.
Attested (v 22): whose identity was proven.
Hades (v 27): here it means the grave, the place of the dead.
Corruption (v 27): referring here to a corpse rotting.
Repent (v 38): literally, means to turn around completely.
Exhort (v 40): strongly urge.

5. How did Peter explain…
   - what had just happened (v 16-21)?

   - who Jesus was (v 22-36)?

   - the right response to the resurrection of the Lord Jesus and the coming of the Spirit (v 37-40)?

Explore More | OPTIONAL

📖 **Read Luke 22:54-62 and John 21:15-19**

- In what sense is Peter himself an embodiment of the truths he is proclaiming about humanity, and about what Christ offers?

6. What was the result of Peter's sermon (v 41)?

7. What was this new-born church, full of 3,000 brand new Christians, like (v 42-47)?

Apply

8. How can your church today learn from the example of the early church here?

Getting Personal | OPTIONAL

Luke is able to use the word "devoted" to describe the approach of these new Christians to the teaching, fellowship, Communion, and prayer of their church.

Could this word be used to describe your approach to your church? Why/why not? Does anything need to change?

Investigate

📖 **Read Acts 3:1-10**

DICTIONARY

Alms (v 3): money; a donation.

9. What was this man hoping for?

- In what sense was he disappointed, and in what sense was he satisfied?

Read Acts 3:11 – 4:4

DICTIONARY

Portico (v 11): entrance porch.
Covenant (v 25): binding agreement.

Sadducees (4:1): a religious group who were very powerful, being well-connected politically.

10. What similarities are there between this sermon and the response to it, and the previous one (2:14-41)?

11. What differences do you notice?

Getting Personal | OPTIONAL

The people were mistakenly looking to the faith and piety of Peter and John as the source of the miracle. Peter, however, repudiated those (surely tempting) accolades (v 12, 16). We, too, ought to deflect praise upwards to the source of all blessings and gifts.

How much do you do this? When are you most tempted to take full credit for the achievements your gifts or abilities supposedly bring?

Apply

12. How do Peter's two evangelistic sermons show us what faithful and effective witness will look like for us?

Pray

Praise God...

- *for the provision of his Spirit. Praise him for the way the Spirit is working in and through you at present.*
- *for the provision of your church. Praise him for the ways in which your church is like this church in Acts 2.*

Ask God...

- *to enable you to be devoted to your church and to its teaching ministry.*
- *to work through you, by his Spirit, to share his gospel. Pray for particular opportunities you have to do this.*

3

Church Challenges

Acts 4:5 - 5:42

The Story So Far...

Jesus tasked his followers with taking the gospel to the end of the earth, before ascending into heaven. His people prayed as they waited for the Spirit.

The Spirit came at Pentecost, enabling God's people to proclaim Christ and call for repentance. Thousands repented and believed, and the church was born.

Talkabout

1. What are the greatest challenges your church faces?

- How do you think they can be overcome (if indeed they can)?

Investigate

📖 **Read Acts 4:5-22**

DICTIONARY

Name (v 12): person, or authority.

Common (v 13): not born into privilege.

2. Read Luke 22:66 – 23:2, 10. Why would Peter and John have had every right to feel terrified in Acts 4:5-7?

3. What does Peter say about Jesus (v 8-12)?

- Why is he able to speak like this in such a setting (v 8)?

Explore More | OPTIONAL

In the Jewish world, the cornerstone was an ornamental stone that identified a building, made it distinctive, and gave it meaning.

📖 **Read Psalm 118:21-24**

- How does Peter's use of verse 22 in Acts 4:11 contain both a solemn warning and a wonderful promise?

📖 **Read Luke 20:9-18**

- How did Jesus himself use the same verse in a similar way?

4. What do Peter and John say about themselves (v 18-20)?

Read Acts 4:23-31

DICTIONARY

Gentiles (v 25, 27): here, meaning those who are not part of Israel.

Anointed (v 26): chosen king. Kings of Israel were anointed with oil.
Predestined (v 28): already decided.

5. How does the church respond to the threats of the religious and political elite?

6. What do we learn here about prayer?

Read Acts 4:32-37

DICTIONARY

Testimony (v 33): true, personal account.
Proceeds (v 34): income.

Levite (v 36): of the Israelite/Jewish tribe of Levi.

7. Other than prayer, what else marked this church?

Getting Personal | OPTIONAL

Material goods fade away. Rejoicing in Christ with his people will last forever.

How is that truth going to direct the way you use, or give away, your "stuff"? What might hold you back?

Apply

8. What would the challenges this church faced look like in your setting?

- What would it look like for your church to respond to those challenges in the way this church did?

Investigate

Read Acts 5:1-16

DICTIONARY

Esteem (v 13): respect.

9. What is the challenge to the church in verses 1-11?

10. How does this passage reveal to us God's view of hypocrisy?

- What do you make of the severity of the punishment here?

Apply

11. What forms might this challenge take in your church today?

- How can you deal with it in a way that is serious but also gracious?

Investigate

📖 **Read Acts 5:17-42**

DICTIONARY

High priest (v 17): the leader of the Jewish religion; one of the most powerful men in Jerusalem.
Bring this man's blood upon us (v 28): hold us responsible for this man's death.
Exalted (v 31): lifted up.
The name (v 41): i.e. Jesus, and his cause.

12. What is challenging to us about the way that the apostles respond to what is done to them (v 41-42)?

Getting Personal | OPTIONAL

Once again, the apostles did not value their own personal security above Jesus' command to witness to him. Do you?

The disciples even rejoiced that they were counted worthy of suffering for the sake of the gospel. Do you?

When we, like they, trust in God's sovereignty and genuinely desire to see the kingdom of God advance, we will not begrudge God's trials in our lives, but we will even learn to rejoice in them.

Does that need to change your perspective, or your conduct or speech, in any way this week?

Pray

Speak to God about the ways in which your church faces the challenges we've seen in this passage.

Spend time asking for his grace so that you can be a church that resists pressure to stay silent about Christ, and resists the temptations of compromise and hypocrisy among yourselves.

4

I See the Heavens Opened

Acts 6:1 - 7:60

The Story So Far...

Jesus tasked his followers with taking the gospel to the end of the earth, before ascending into heaven. His people prayed as they waited for the Spirit.

The Spirit came at Pentecost, enabling God's people to proclaim Christ and call for repentance. Thousands repented and believed, and the church was born.

The church overcame external pressure to be silent about Jesus, and internal temptation to live hypocritically, praying for boldness to continue preaching Christ.

Talkabout

1. What do you think it would take for you to be willing to die for your faith?

Investigate

📖 **Read Acts 6:1-7**

DICTIONARY

Hellenists (v 1): Greek-speaking Jewish Christians.

Hebrews (v 1): Aramaic-speaking Jewish Christians.

2. What was the challenge facing the church, and how was it resolved?

3. How do the apostles prioritize word ministry without neglecting mercy ministry?

Explore More | OPTIONAL

📖 **Read 1 Timothy 3:1-7**

What are the qualifications for being an "overseer"—that is, an elder or a pastor?

📖 **Read 1 Timothy 3:8-13**

- What are the qualifications for being a deacon—serving the church through practical ministry as these seven men in Acts 6 did?
- What differences do you see?
- How do these lists underline the importance of both ministries?
- How do they move us to pray for both our pastors/elders and our deacons (whether these are formal or informal roles)?

Getting Personal | OPTIONAL

How are you encouraging your pastors to spend their time in the ministry of the word and of prayer?

How are you serving your church, either through word ministry or practical ministry? What could you do differently?

4. In what way is Stephen introduced to us here?

Read Acts 6:8-15

DICTIONARY

Withstand (v 10): argue successfully against.
Instigated (v 11): prompted.
Blasphemous (v 11): dishonoring to God. This was punishable by death.
This holy place (v 13): the Jerusalem Temple.

5. How does Luke continue to build a portrait of Stephen in these verses?

6. Why did his opponents resort to underhand means?

Verse 15 is rather perplexing—what did Stephen look like? In the Bible, angels are not sweet, adorable creatures, seeking to bring cuteness to a room. They are messengers of God. They inspire awe and fear. Their purpose is to bring a message from the one true God.

Thus for Luke to say that Stephen had the face of an angel is to comment on his role as a true messenger of the word of God. Luke is not asking us to picture Stephen with what we imagine to be a cherub-like face, but rather with an expression that denoted his determination to speak God's word fearlessly, faithfully, and forcefully, to the end.

Apply

7. "Effective evangelism will lead to great fruit." Discuss, from this passage.

- What are the implications for our own everyday witness?

Investigate

Read Acts 7:1-60

DICTIONARY

Mesopotamia (v 2): modern-day Iraq.
Kindred (v 3): family.
Sojourners (v 6): guests; temporary dwellers.
Twelve patriarchs (v 8): Jacob's sons, who gave their names to the twelve tribes of Israel.
Expose (v 19): here, meaning leave outside to die.
Oracles (v 38): revelations; words.
Aaron (v 40): Moses' brother.
Moloch, Rephan (v 43): false gods worshiped by peoples near Israel.
Stiff-necked (v 51): having necks that won't bow in worship.
Son of Man (v 56): Jesus, in all his heavenly glory (Daniel 7:13-14).

Stephen was accused of speaking against two sacred aspects of 1st-century Jewish life: the law and the temple. There were no more grievous charges to lay against a Jew, and it became a familiar tactic of the Jewish opponents of the early church. (See Acts 18:12-13; 21:27-32.)

8. How does Stephen rebut these accusations?
   - Speaking against Moses and the law (7:35-40, 52-53)

   - Speaking against God's temple (which was the place of God's presence among his people. Think about what Stephen is teaching his audience about God's presence in verses 2, 9, 30-33, 44-50.)

9. What picture does Stephen's unfolding of Old Testament history give us…
   - of God?

   - of God's people through the Old Testament?

10. What is Stephen's conclusion about his listeners, and what is their conclusion about him (v 51-58)?

11. What do Stephen's last three utterances teach us about dying well (v 55-60)?

Apply

12. What did Stephen know that enabled him to live as he did and die as he did?

    - What would it take for you to be willing to live like that, and (if called to) to die like that?

Getting Personal | OPTIONAL

Our God reigns. Even if the world turns against us, we will find Jesus standing in heaven, ready to receive us as we remain faithful to him.

What difference will that make to the way you live this week?

Who could you ask to hold you accountable for actually living out the way you answered that question?

Pray

Use your answers to question 12 to guide your prayers.

Finish your time together by praying for the persecuted church around the world (csw.org.uk and/or opendoorsusa.org will help you to pray in an informed way).

5

Beyond Jerusalem

Acts 8:1-40

The Story So Far...

Jesus tasked his followers with taking the gospel to the end of the earth. The Spirit came at Pentecost, thousands repented, and the church was born.

The church overcame external pressure to be silent about Jesus, and internal temptation to live hypocritically, praying for boldness to continue preaching Christ.

Stephen lived to serve the church and share the gospel before dying for the faith as the first Christian martyr. He saw Jesus in heaven, standing to welcome him.

Talkabout

1. Have you ever experienced a terrible situation from which great good resulted?

    - Did that experience cause you to look differently at life in any way? How?

Investigate

Read Acts 8:1-8

2. What state did the church seem to be in by the end of verse 3?

- What state did the church seem to be in by the end of verse 8?

Getting Personal | OPTIONAL

The message of the gospel was received "with much joy."

Recall your own conversion. How did you experience the joy of discovering who Jesus was and coming under his rule?

How might you recall that joy each day, so that it continues to be a mark of your life?

3. Read John 4:7-9. How does this context make the growth of the church in Samaria all the more wonderful?

Read Acts 8:9-25

DICTIONARY

Gall (v 23): resentment; bile.
Bond (v 23): chain.
Iniquity (v 23): sin.

When the apostles arrived, they laid their hands on the Samaritan believers and they received the Holy Spirit (v 17). This was Samaria's Pentecost moment, and it demonstrated that the church at Jerusalem and the church at Samaria constituted one people of God.

4. What was Simon's status before Philip arrived?

- What did Simon desire after Philip and the apostles had arrived (v 18-20)?

- What did Peter identify as Simon's problem (v 21-23)?

Explore More | OPTIONAL

- If you had been there at the end of verse 13, what would you have made of Simon?

We need to recognize that simply because someone says they believe in the Lord Jesus Christ, it does not necessarily mean they are genuinely converted.

📖 **Read Matthew 7:21-23; 13:18-23 and James 2:14-19**

- What do Jesus and James say are the real signs of a truly converted heart?

As the Reformer John Calvin put it, it is faith alone that saves, but the faith that saves is never alone. Simon's "faith" showed itself to be false in his self-serving efforts to buy power. True faith shows itself to be genuine in its obedience and love for Christ's people.

Apply

5. What should the spread of the church into Samaria teach your church today?

6. How should the example of Simon warn us as believers today?

Investigate

The first half of Acts 8 shows how *not* to respond to the gospel. Simon wanted the benefits of the gospel but would not truly submit his life to King Jesus. The second half of Acts 8 shows us a genuine picture of conversion.

📖 **Read Acts 8:26-40**

7. What does Luke tell us about the man in the chariot (v 27-28)?

Jewish law did not permit this man, as a eunuch, to enter the Jerusalem Temple. He could watch and worship from a distance in the Court of Gentiles, but he could not enter the Court of Israel. Even if he'd been a Jew, his status as a eunuch would still have rendered him unacceptable.

8. What role in this unlikely conversion is played by…
    - the word of God?

    - a servant of God?

9. What does this episode teach us about the Old Testament?

10. What suggests that the eunuch's conversion was genuine (v 36-39)?

11. What reasons could Philip have come up with for not preaching the gospel at various points in this chapter?

    - What would he not have experienced if he had given up at each of those points?

Getting Personal | OPTIONAL

What causes you to be tempted to give up witnessing to the truth about Jesus among those you live and work with?

What truths about God will you use to counter these temptations?

Apply

12. How should this chapter lead us to think about the possibility of Christians being persecuted in our culture or country?

Pray

Share as many of your answers to the Getting Personal section, above, as you are comfortable with, and use them as a basis for prayers of confession and prayers asking God to apply gospel truths to your lives.

Finish by praising God that the gospel knows no boundaries.

6

The Most Unlikely Conversion

Acts 9:1-43

The Story So Far...

Jesus tasked his followers with taking the gospel to the end of the earth. The Spirit came at Pentecost, thousands repented, and the church was born.

Stephen lived to serve the church and share the gospel before dying for the faith as the first Christian martyr. He saw Jesus in heaven, standing to welcome him.

The persecution and scattering of the church was used by God to grow his kingdom into Samaria, and to bring an Ethiopian eunuch to joyful saving faith.

Talkabout

1. Of the people you know, who do you consider least likely to become a Christian? Why?

Investigate

📖 **Read Acts 9:1-9**

DICTIONARY

Damascus (v 2): see map on page 6.

2. Why was Saul such an unlikely convert to Christianity? (v 1-2; see also 7:58 – 8:3.)

3. How does Jesus describe the relationship between Saul and himself (Acts 9:4-5)?

    - What does this tell us about the relationship between Jesus and his church?

📖 **Read Acts 9:10-22**

DICTIONARY

Saints (v 13): believers.
Instrument (v 15): tool; agent.
Carry my name (v 15): proclaim who I am.
Confounded (v 22): stunned; defeated.

4. What is impressive about Ananias' obedience here?

5. What does the Lord reveal about his plans for Saul (v 15-16)?

6. Why were the residents of Damascus right to be "amazed" (v 21)?

Getting Personal | OPTIONAL

The persecutor of the gospel had become a proclaimer of it, having been broken by Christ. As he himself put it later, "God chose what is foolish in the world to shame the wise; God chose what is weak in the world to shame the strong" (1 Corinthians 1:27).

Do you embrace or deny your weakness?

Are you truly willing to be known as a fool because of your faith?

Saul believed, and so he spoke. Do you?

Explore More | OPTIONAL

Read Philippians 3:4-11 and 2 Corinthians 11:22-29

- What was life like for Saul/Paul before he was converted, and after?
- How do his words in Philippians show that it was worth giving up all that he had in order to suffer all that he endured?

Apply

7. How should God's sovereign power in converting people encourage us in our own prayers and witness?

Investigate

📖 **Read Acts 9:23-31**

DICTIONARY

Hellenists (v 29): here, meaning Greek-speaking Jews.

Fear (v 31): here, meaning great awe.

God had promised that he would "show [Paul] how much he must suffer for the sake of my name" (v 16).

8. How does Paul begin to be shown this here?

📖 **Read Acts 9:32-43**

9. What are the similarities between the events of 9:36-43 and Luke 8:40-56?

- What are the similarities and differences between the events of Acts 9:36-43 and what Paul writes in 1 Corinthians 15:51-53?

10. What was the outcome both of Saul's conversion and ministry (v 31), and Peter's signs and ministry (v 35, 42)?

11. How are lives changed in Acts 9, and by what means?

Apply

12. What have we learned about true discipleship from...
    - Saul?
    - Ananias?

- Barnabas?

Getting Personal | OPTIONAL

In what ways are you most like these men? And in which way least?

How could reflecting on the power and mercy of God transform you to be more like them?

Pray

Look back on your pre-conversion life (if you can remember it) and thank God for the ways in which he has changed you, in salvation and in transforming you into his Son's likeness.

Give thanks for particular people who spoke gospel truth into your life.

Use your answers to question 12 to ask God to shape you into faithful, effective, loving disciples.

7

To the Gentiles

Acts 10:1 - 11:30

The Story So Far...

Jesus tasked his followers with taking the gospel to the end of the earth. The Spirit came at Pentecost, thousands repented, and the church was born.

The persecution and scattering of the church was used by God to grow his kingdom into Samaria, and to bring an Ethiopian eunuch to joyful saving faith.

Saul, the church's chief persecutor, was converted by Christ and turned into one of its foremost preachers, welcomed into the church by forgiving Christians.

Talkabout

1. What is your church's reputation among other like-minded churches? If they had to sum up your church in three words or phrases, what would they be, do you think?

Investigate

📖 **Read Acts 10:1-33**

DICTIONARY

Italian Cohort (v 1): a prestigious Roman army unit.
Lodging (v 18): staying.
God-fearing man (v 22): a non-Jew who worshiped the God of Israel.

2. What do we learn about Cornelius in verses 1-2?

3. Trace the path of events that leads to Peter visiting Cornelius in Caesarea.
   - v 3-8
   - v 9-16
   - v 17-20

- v 21-23

- v 24-29

- v 30-33

Explore More | OPTIONAL

- Based on what Peter says to God, what kinds of animals did the sheets in Peter's vision clearly contain (v 12-14)?

Read Leviticus 11:1-47

- Why is Peter's response to being told, "kill and eat" understandable?

These laws had two purposes. One purpose was health, but the other—the more important purpose—was to distinguish Israel as God's people. Israel was to be distinct, not only by how they worshiped but also by what they ate. This was a sign of commitment to the one true and living God. Yet, Peter sees all kinds of four-footed animals in his vision. That includes clean animals and unclean ones, such as pigs, reptiles, and other animals that crawl on the earth.

- Given the purpose of these laws, what is God teaching Peter here, do you think?

4. Why was Peter's presence in Cornelius' house in itself a strange occurrence (v 27-28)?

Getting Personal | OPTIONAL

Don't underestimate how uncomfortable God's command to Peter was. Yet Peter still obeyed. Similarly, God will ask of us things that require us to go outside of our comfort zone. We are called to obey, even when we are perplexed.

How are you allowing the Lord to lead you out of your comfort zone to do his work at the moment? Why is this an exciting way to live?

Read Acts 10:34-48

DICTIONARY

Partiality (v 34): favoritism; bias.

Extolling (v 46): praising.

5. How did Peter connect his vision with his Spirit-given command to go and see Cornelius (v 28-29, 34-35)?

Peter has realized that "in every nation anyone who fears [God] and does what is right is acceptable to him" (v 35).

6. What does it mean to fear God and do what is right (v 35), according to verses 36-43?

7. How do verses 44-48 show that Peter was right—that the gospel was breaking through another barrier, to the Gentiles?

Apply

8. What did Peter need to understand and then do in order to be in a position to declare the gospel to these Gentiles?

- What are the lessons of this for you as individuals and as a church?

Investigate

📖 **Read Acts 11:1-30**

DICTIONARY

Circumcision party (v 2): Christians who were very concerned that God's people keep God's law and remain clearly separate from those who did not worship Jesus.

Grace (v 23): undeserved, overflowing kindness.

Relief (v 29): help.

9. What is at stake—for us too, 2,000 years later—in verses 2-18?

Getting Personal | OPTIONAL

Notice that those who had been critical of Peter (v 2) fell silent (v 18) and then "glorified God." What a transformation! They were willing to change their minds and retract their opinions based on Peter's testimony regarding God's word. Are you?

When was the last time you changed your mind on something important to you and how you live, based on what you saw, or were shown, in God's word?

Explore More | OPTIONAL

Before moving on, it is worth asking the question: how should Christians think about circumcision?

Read Colossians 2:8-14

- How does this passage help us?

10. How do events in Antioch mirror Peter's visit to Caesarea, and extend what was happening there (v 19-26)?

11. How does the church—now made up of Jewish and Gentile local churches—display its unity (v 27-30)?

Apply

The church in Antioch was known for its witness to non-Christians (v 20-22), for its loyalty to Christ (v 26), and for its generosity toward other believers (v 29).

12. To what extent are these qualities things that your church is known for?

- How about you personally?

Pray

Thank God...

- *that the gospel is for all people, including you.*
- *for your church, and for all the ways in which it is a faithful, loving, generous, witnessing community.*

Pray for your church...

- *that God would continue to show you how you might be more and more the community of people he has called you to be.*

Pray for yourselves...

- *that you would be quick to allow God to lead you out of your comfort zone in order to share the gospel. Pray about particular ways in which you are being challenged to do this.*
- *that you would be actively contributing to the life of your church, in order to enable it to be more and more like the church in Antioch.*

8

The Apostle, the Angel, and the King

Acts 12:1-25

The Story So Far...

Jesus tasked his followers with taking the gospel to the end of the earth. The Spirit came at Pentecost, thousands repented, and the church was born.

Saul, the church's chief persecutor, was converted by Christ and turned into one of its foremost preachers, welcomed into the church by forgiving Christians.

Through Peter, the gospel came to Cornelius, a Roman centurion. The Jerusalem church praised God for this; the church in Antioch saw many Gentile converts.

Talkabout

1. Which person on earth has the most influence or power over your life?

Investigate

Read Acts 12:1-4

DICTIONARY

Unleavened Bread (v 3): another name for the Passover festival.

We meet many Herods in the Bible. This particular Herod was Herod Agrippa, the grandson of Herod the Great, who tried to kill Jesus soon after he was born (Matthew 2:1-18). Herod Agrippa claimed to be a Jew (his grandmother was Jewish). This enabled him to tell his masters in Rome that he was able to keep the peace. He moved to live in Jerusalem and visited the temple each day.

2. What new way did he now find to curry favor with the Jews (v 1-4)?

Read Acts 12:5-17

3. How did the church react to Peter's imprisonment?

- How did God respond to Peter's imprisonment?

4. Given that the Christians were praying for Peter's release, what is strange about their reaction to him standing on the doorstep in verses 13-16?

Apply

5. Read Colossians 4:2. What does Paul tell us we should be when it comes to our prayers?

- How can you avoid the mistake of the Christians in Acts 12, and instead be "watchful"?

- How would being watchful both motivate and shape your prayers, do you think?

Investigate

Read Acts 12:18-25

DICTIONARY

King's chamberlain (v 20): an important position, enjoying influential access to the king.

Caesarea (v 19) was the least Jewish city in the area.

6. What do you think was the significance of Herod locating himself there, instead of in Jerusalem?

7. What do Tyre and Sidon ask Herod for, and why (v 20)?

As Herod sits on his throne to give his decision, Luke does not tell us the content of his speech (v 21). Instead, he focuses on the crowd's response.

8. What was that response (v 22)?

9. What happened next, and why (v 23)?

- How does the man who had escaped Herod's clutches show us the right response to receiving praise and honor? (See 3:12-16; 10:25-26.)

Explore More | OPTIONAL

Read Psalm 8

- How does a right view of God, and of ourselves, cause us to live with...
  - right humility?
  - great dignity?
- Given the truths of this psalm, what would it look like to...
  - make too little of ourselves?
  - make too much of ourselves?

Getting Personal | OPTIONAL

When we recognize that Christ is the greatest treasure in earth and heaven, we will gladly forgo the accolades of men to see God's glory made more visible and more fully known.

To what extent is Christ your greatest treasure? How is this seen in your own response to praise (or to its lack)?

---

10. Herod was a powerful, influential king. What does the inclusion of Acts 12:24 remind us about human power and God's plans?

11. This is the last session in this first study guide to Acts. Sum up in a couple of sentences the ways in which the church has been transformed in twelve chapters.

Apply

12. How have the first twelve chapters of Acts given you...
    - a greater awe of God?
    - an increased reliance on and joy in his indwelling Spirit?

- a more committed attitude toward your church?

- a greater confidence in evangelism?

Getting Personal | OPTIONAL

God's Spirit always works through God's word to change God's people.

How has he prompted you to change through your time in Acts 1 – 12?

Are you embracing and pursuing that change prayerfully and joyfully or are you resisting that or being grudging about doing it?

Pray

Use your answers to question 12 to...

- *praise God for who he is and what he has done.*
- *pray for your own lives and witness.*

Acts 1–12

The Church Is Born

LEADER'S GUIDE

Leader's Guide: Introduction

This Leader's Guide includes guidance for every question. It will provide background information and help you if you get stuck. For each session, you'll also find the following:

The Big Idea: The main point of the session, in brief. This is what you should be aiming to have fixed in people's minds by the end of the session!

Summary: An overview of the passage you're reading together.

Optional Extra: Usually this is an introductory activity that ties in with the main theme of the Bible study and is designed to break the ice at the beginning of a session. Or it may be a "homework project" that people can tackle during the week.

Occasionally the Leader's Guide includes an extra follow-up question, printed in ***italics***. This doesn't appear in the main study guide but could be a useful add-on to help your group get to the answer or go deeper.

Here are a few key principles to bear in mind as you prepare to lead:

- Don't just read out the answers from the Leader's Guide. Ideally, you want the group to discover these answers from the Bible for themselves.
- Keep drawing people back to the passage you're studying. People may come up with answers based on their experiences or on teaching they've heard in the past, but the point of this study is to listen to God's word itself—so keep directing your group to look at the text.
- Make sure everyone finishes the session knowing how the passage is relevant for them. We do Bible study so that our lives can be changed by what we hear from God's word. So, **Apply** questions aren't just an add-on—they're a vital part of the session.

Finally, remember that your group is unique! You should feel free to use this Good Book Guide in a way that works for them. If they're a quiet bunch, you might want to spend longer on the **Talkabout** question. If they love to get creative, try using mind-mapping or doodling to kick-start some of your discussions. If your time is limited, you can choose to skip **Explore More** or split the whole session into two. Adapt the material in whatever way you think will help your group get the most out of God's word.

1

Promises

Acts 1:1-26

The Big Idea

Through the presence of the Spirit and the reliable witness of the apostles, we have everything we need to obey Jesus' command to proclaim his gospel to the end of the earth.

Summary

The book of Acts begins the same way as the Gospel of Luke, showing that this is the second volume of Luke's two-volume history. In Acts 1:1–2, Luke reminds Theophilus that the first volume is dedicated to "all that Jesus began to do and teach, until the day when he was taken up, after he had given commands through the Holy Spirit to the apostles." Luke also indicates the content of Jesus' teaching during the time after the resurrection but before Christ's ascension. Jesus was "speaking about the kingdom of God" (v 3). This mention of the kingdom of God is significant. As the rest of Acts unfolds, much of the preaching in the book focuses on the coming of God's kingdom in the person of Christ. In fact, not only does the book of Acts begin with God's kingdom; it also ends with Paul declaring the kingdom of God (Acts 28:31).

Acts 1:8 is one of the most important verses in the book. First, it shows us that the power the Holy Spirit gives to God's people is the power to witness to Christ. Second, this verse also functions as a second "Great Commission." Jesus describes the gospel moving out through concentric circles from Jerusalem to Judea and Samaria, and finally to the entire world—which means this commission applies to us too. This verse functions as a preview of the entire book of Acts, which will track the movement of the apostles as they travel from Jerusalem to the outer reaches of the Roman Empire.

Having given this commission, Jesus ascends back to heaven, and two angels assure his followers that he will one day return (v 9-11). In the meantime, they have their marching orders in verse 8. But first, they must wait for the Spirit. As they do so, they unite in fellowship and prayer (v 12-14). Luke then further details the events of the upper room where they met, particularly as they pertain to the leadership of the early church. Peter's address to the other disciples focuses on Judas' betrayal of Christ. As he speaks, Peter clearly teaches first, the prophetic nature of the Old Testament—it had to be fulfilled (v 16)—and second, the authorship of Scripture as being both divine and human (v 16).

Peter's concern is to appoint an apostle to replace Judas, and the qualifications for an apostle are given in verses 21-22. Supremely, he must be "a witness to

[Christ's] resurrection" (v 22). We should take tremendous comfort from the fact that our faith is not based on hearsay, rumor, or wishful thinking. Instead our faith is based on the historical fact of the resurrection of Christ—an event substantiated by hundreds of eyewitnesses in the early church, including the apostles themselves (1 Corinthians 15:6).

Optional Extra

Split your group into pairs. Give one person in each pair a photograph. They must describe the photo and give step-by-step instructions so that their partner can draw it without seeing it for themselves. When time is up, compare pictures and ask which group member was the most "faithful witness" to the photo in front of them. This links to the apostles' role in being faithful witnesses to all that they saw and heard about Jesus, and is a fun way to build relationships.

Guidance for Questions

1. **What is the hardest thing you have ever been asked to do?**
- **Did you back out or did you take it on? If the latter, were you successful, and why?**
  Do not allow people's stories to go on too long! The aim is simply to introduce the idea that life throws up hard challenges that sometimes we may duck but at other times we must take on. We return to this theme at the end of the study, by which stage the group will have seen that the Lord Jesus asks us to do a very hard thing, as he did his first followers—but he also, by his Spirit and in his word, gives us the means to do it.

2. **How does Luke describe what he recounted in "the first book"—the Gospel of Luke (v 1-2)?**
   Luke reminds Theophilus that the first volume was dedicated to "all that Jesus began to do and teach, until the day when he was taken up, after he had given commands through the Holy Spirit to the apostles." Notice the word "began," which implies that Acts is the record of what Jesus continued to do and to teach, by the Spirit, in his church, after his ascension into heaven (which Luke recounts in Acts 1:9-11).

3. **What did Jesus do after he had risen (v 3)?**
   - "By many proofs" and many appearances, he showed that he truly had risen from the dead.
   - He spoke "about the kingdom of God." This mention of the kingdom of God is significant. As the rest of Acts unfolds, we will find that much of the apostles' teaching focuses on the coming of God's kingdom in the person of Christ. In fact, the book finishes with Paul "proclaiming the kingdom of God" (28:31).

So this was the summary of Jesus' message—that he had truly risen, and was therefore the King of God's kingdom, which in his death he had opened for all to enter and enjoy.

4. **What did Jesus tell his apostles…**

- **they must do (v 4-5)?**
  Wait in Jerusalem until the Holy Spirit came upon them. The mark of a true Christian is that they have received the Spirit, just as the mark of a follower of John the Baptist was water baptism. A Christian's water baptism is the outer sign of the inner reality that they have received the Spirit.

- **they must be (v 8)?**
  Witnesses. As a witness in a court of law is charged to tell the truth of what they know, so the apostles were charged with proclaiming the truth of Christ. This verse might be one of the most important in the book of Acts. First, it shows us that the power the Holy Spirit gives to God's people is the power to witness to Christ. Second, it functions as a second "Great Commission" (Matthew 28:18-20). Jesus describes the gospel moving out through concentric circles from Jerusalem to Judea and Samaria, and finally to the entire world.

5. **Imagine you were one of those first followers, in a city that killed your King and hates your message. How would you have felt hearing verse 8?**
   Answers to this question will depend partly on individuals' personalities. The more confident, can-do people may have felt that this was a great challenge to be met, and so started planning their missions campaign. Most of us, I guess, would be far more fearful and reticent, and wonder whether this was a realistic idea or even a fair command to give. The church was a few dozen nobodies, facing a Jewish elite who hated their Master and a Roman Empire whose soldiers had killed him with a message about a crucified Savior. How could that ever reach the end of the earth?

   Of course, some may reflect that, by trusting Jesus' promise of power through the Spirit, they would have felt afraid but also hopeful. There are no wrong answers here—the aim is to encourage your group to place themselves in the shoes of those first Christians as they received this commission.

6. **After Jesus ascended back to heaven, what did the angels (the "two men … in white robes") most want his followers to know (v 10-11)?**
   That just as Jesus ascended into heaven, so also he will one day descend in glory and power at the second coming. In the physical absence of Jesus, his followers needed (and need still today) to retain the ever-present thought that Jesus will one day return to fully establish his kingdom.

Explore More

- ***What do these passages teach us about the significance of the ascension?***
- ***Philippians 2:6-11***
  Jesus is now seated in the highest place, worthy of the greatest praise, and one day will hear every single person confess his true identity.
- ***Ephesians 1:20-23***
  Because Jesus ascended into heaven through the power of God, he is now reigning from the throne of God. Though Jesus is absent physically from the church, he is actively ruling over his church from his place at the right hand of God.
- ***Hebrews 4:14-16; 7:23-25***
  Christ has now become the mediator of those who believe in him. As the author of Hebrews asserts, Christ became every believer's superior great High Priest: one who can both sympathize with us in our humanity and also speak for us in his divinity; and he is currently interceding for his church in heaven.

---

7. **What difference should it make to us to remember that "this Jesus ... will come in the same way as [the apostles] saw him go" (v 11)?**
   All the difference! Your group may come up with some or all of these things, or others:
   - It gives us hope when life is hard.
   - It gives urgency to our proclamation of his kingdom.
   - It encourages us to live lives of holiness.
   - It reminds us that history has an end-point.
   - It causes us to remember that eternity is more important than this life.
   - It gives perspective to our triumphs and our trials.

   You may like to pause here to give thanks that Jesus will return.

8. **What part do we have to play in the "Great Commission" of verse 8?**
   The gospel witness has not yet reached "the end of the earth." We are now tasked with witnessing to the truth we know about Christ, just as our forefathers in the faith were, for the task is as yet unfinished. This may take us overseas to an unreached people group, or it may take us over the road to an unconverted neighbor, but it will take us somewhere. All of us are called to witness to Christ and to seek to make disciples of all nations, including our own, until the Lord Jesus returns.

- **What happens if we forget about the role of the Holy Spirit in this?**
  We will either be self-reliant, and become proud if we are "good witnesses" or crushed when we fail; or, overcome by our own weakness and fears, we will never witness at all.
- **What difference does it make if we know we have received his power?**
  We will be bold and courageous, knowing that the Spirit's power is at work in us to help us speak and to use what we are able to speak to bring

glory to the Son. We shall not conclude that we cannot speak clearly enough or answer questions well enough; nor that particular people are "unconvertible." We will also be humble, knowing that it is only by his power that our words are uttered, and effectual. When we witness and meet with rejection, we shall not give up; when we witness and it results in real interest or even in conversion, we shall praise God.

9. **What did these Christians do while they waited for the Spirit (v 12-14)?**
   The group as a whole joined together "with one accord." At the simplest level, the point is that they spent time gathered together as they waited. Moreover, Luke is affirming that everyone present was committed to the unifying belief that Christ was the Messiah, risen from the dead, and ascended into heaven. Faith in Jesus unified them together as one people. And as they waited, they devoted themselves to prayer (v 14). Trusting in the promise of the coming Holy Spirit, the group looked to God in prayer to guide their actions.

- ***OPTIONAL: Read Mark 3:21 and John 7:5. Why is Acts 1:14 significant?***
  Throughout the Gospels, Jesus' family are placed in opposition to Jesus and his ministry—Mark even notes that Jesus' own family thought he was "out of his mind" (Mark 3:21); and John states, "Not even his brothers believed in him" (John 7:5). Now however, Jesus' family—his mother Mary and his brothers—is counted among this small band of faithful believers in the upper room. It is a great reminder that the gospel is capable of changing literally anyone. In the same way that Jesus' brothers came to believe in him after denying his identity and straying from his teaching, so too can the vilest and most ungodly come to Christ.

10. **What do verses 15-26 teach us about...**
    - **what happened to Judas after he betrayed Jesus?**
      Judas used the betrayal money—30 pieces of silver (Matthew 26:14-15)—to buy property. Without any further explanation as to the cause of the incident, Luke describes Judas as "falling headlong," after which, "he burst open in the middle and all his bowels gushed out." This is both vivid and horrifying, but worse is the implication in verse 25 that Judas went "to his own place," the place of torment beyond death for those who die in rebellion against Christ. This is a sobering reminder and challenge to all professing Christians—see the Getting Personal section below question 10 in the Study Guide.
    - **the Old Testament Scriptures?**
      - Peter indicates that the Scripture "had to be fulfilled" (v 16). This statement shows Peter's confidence in the veracity of Scripture and in the prophetic nature of the Old Testament.

- Peter indicates that Scripture came as "the Holy Spirit spoke beforehand by the mouth of David." Thus, Peter simultaneously affirms the divine and human authorship of Scripture. God speaks in Scripture, but he speaks through certain individuals. As Peter wrote later in his second epistle, "Men spoke from God as they were carried along by the Holy Spirit" (2 Peter 1:21). Thus, when Scripture speaks, God speaks.

- **the qualifications for being an apostle?**
  Peter stressed the importance of the future apostle being one who was present during Jesus' ministry and a witness to his resurrection (v 21-22). The new disciple had to have been present from "the baptism of John" to the day Jesus "was taken up from us" (i.e. his ascension), so that he could be a "witness with us of his resurrection." Thus, the twelfth apostle must be a man who was present from the beginning of Christ's ministry until the end.

  NOTE: Verse 26 raises the question: should we cast lots today for important decisions? I do not believe we should. We must remember to interpret Scripture according to its own historical timeline. As the history of God's plan to redeem his people moves from one epoch (or stage) to another, so too do the expectations on God's people. Since we live after the coming of the Holy Spirit (Acts 2) and the completion of the canon of Scripture, Christians should now make decisions on the basis of the Spirit's guiding and the teaching of Scripture. We use Bible-informed wisdom in the context of a local church community in order to make faithful, God-honoring decisions.

11. **How do these verses encourage us to rely on the Old Testament Scripture and the apostles' teaching (that is the New Testament)?**
    The Old Testament was inspired by the Spirit, authored by him through a variety of people; and the New Testament was written by the apostles or those who knew them well, and those apostles were men who had been with Jesus during his ministry, seen Jesus after his resurrection, and received his Spirit to guide them. Therefore we can have utter assurance that what we are reading is what God wishes us to read, that it is all that he wishes to reveal to us, and that it is all inspired by his Spirit and inerrantly true.

- **What would true reliance on their authority look like in our day-to-day-lives?**
  We would read the Scriptures, not out of mere duty but out of joy that we can read God's truth. And we would take understanding them seriously, and pray hard that we would see how to obey them in our specific circumstances. And then we would obey them in every way we could, and be quick to repent when we did not.

12. **How will you encourage each other to take on the hard but Spirit-enabled challenge of taking the gospel message "to the end of the earth"? What will that mean for each of you this week?**
It is easy to make excuses for each other about our gospel witness, or to spend so long telling one another that it is hard (by which we mean *too* hard) that we talk ourselves out of ever doing it. We need to remind one another that this is our mission, our Christ-given commission; and that his Spirit is with us, so that we have no need to duck out, nor any excuse for ducking out. We need to be praying for one another, and for those we have opportunity to speak with. We need to be encouraging one another to pray for and give to missionaries who are reaching the lost elsewhere. And we need to be holding one another accountable in our shared commission to take the gospel to the end of the earth.

2

The Spirit-Fueled Church

Acts 2:1 - 4:4

The Big Idea

The Spirit who arrived at Pentecost lives in every believer and gifts them to be devoted to the word of God and to the people of God, and to effectively proclaim the gospel of Jesus Christ.

Summary

By Acts 2, the apostles, along with 120 other disciples and eyewitnesses of Jesus Christ, have gathered in the upper room. They are waiting for the Holy Spirit, whom Christ had promised to send (Acts 1:6-11). Acts 2 describes the fulfillment of that promise on the day of Pentecost as the Holy Spirit descends on the apostles and empowers them for gospel ministry.

Pentecost was the day on which the Holy Spirit was poured out on the disciples (2:1-4). This event is one of perhaps the three most important moments in redemptive history. The first event was creation, the moment when God created the stage on which he would work out his sovereign plan. The second was the substitutionary death and resurrection of the Lord Jesus. In the cross and resurrection of Christ, God accomplished redemption and ushered in the new covenant, fulfilling all the promises and expectations of the Old Testament. The third event is the day of Pentecost—the birth of the church, the creation of God's new-covenant people.

Acts 2 details...

- the coming of the Spirit in a sudden, universal, polarizing way (v 1-13).
- the Spirit-empowered preaching of the gospel by Peter (v 14-36), declaring the fulfillment of prophecy in the coming of the Spirit, and the identity and work of Jesus Christ; and calling for a response of repentance and baptism (v 37-41).
- the nature of the first church, which was devoted to the apostolic teaching, as well as to fellowship, to prayer, and to the Lord's Supper, and which grew quickly by God's grace (v 42-47).

People of all walks of life were repenting and being baptized, and the Lord was adding to their number daily—this is the true miracle of Acts 2. And that miracle continues today, in every local church that is moved by the Spirit to gather round the word, that lives in awe of the Lord, and that therefore proclaims the gospel to all who will hear.

This study also looks, more briefly, at Acts 3. There, Peter and John, having been used by Christ to heal a lame man, take the opportunity to preach the gospel once more, again causing thousands to turn to Christ, but also arousing opposition (4:1-4). Effective witness is Christ-centered and Christ-exalting, calls for a response, and will be met with both repentance and resistance.

Optional Extra

Ask your group to share the one or two most important turning points or "watershed moments" in their lives when life changed significantly and irrevocably. Alternatively, ask people to draw those moments, and see if the rest of the group can guess what they are referring to.

Guidance for Questions

1. **What makes a good church? How would you answer that question in one or two sentences?**
   It may help your group members to write down their answer before they share it with the rest of the group. There are no wrong answers at this stage, and the question can be well answered in a variety of ways. This passage will give you much insight into the Bible's answer (though there is, of course, more to be said). You would profit from returning to this question after question 7 or 8, or at the end of the study.

2. **Read Ezekiel 37:1-14 and Exodus 19:9, 16-25. How do these verses help us grasp the significance of the sound like wind and the tongues as of fire that demonstrated the coming of the Spirit?**
   - *Wind*: Throughout the Bible, the work of God is described with the imagery of wind. In the Old Testament the Hebrew word *ruach* means both "wind" and "spirit." In Ezekiel 37, the prophet describes the Spirit of God working in and

through the wind. Ezekiel is shown a valley of dry bones and is asked if the bones can live. God then demonstrates his power to Ezekiel by giving the bones muscle and tendons, but even then the bones do not come alive. They only come alive when "breath" from the "four winds" enters them (v 9-10). In verses 13-14, God makes clear this is a symbol for the coming of his Spirit and the life-giving work of that Spirit. By describing the great rushing wind in Acts 2, Luke is indicating that God's life-giving Spirit has come to rest on the apostles.

- *Fire*: In Exodus 19, the people whom God has rescued from Egypt are camped at the foot of Mount Sinai, and the Lord descends to its peak. His presence is made manifest "in fire" (Exodus 19:18). Fire is often the sign of God's presence (see also Exodus 3)—and so it is here in Acts 2. But in the Old Testament, the fire is always an unapproachable one, for sinners cannot approach the holy God and live. Here at Pentecost, by his Spirit, God is present in all his holiness—yet, as those redeemed and cleansed by Jesus' death, these believers can enjoy his presence rather than trembling in fear at it.

3. Who did the event affect in...

- **Acts 2:1-4?**
The "they" in verse 1 refers to the group of believers who were waiting for the Spirit's coming, as the Lord had instructed them (1:4-5). The Spirit came to every Christian.

- **v 5-11?**
Verse 5 tells us that devout men from every nation were gathered in Jerusalem for the Jewish festival of Pentecost. The sound of the rushing wind was so arresting that a multitude gathered to witness the preaching of the apostles. What was even more arresting, however, was that the crowd found the apostles speaking in different languages (or tongues, v 6). The global dimension of this event is magnified by the list of nations mentioned in verses 9-11—people from all these nations were caught up in the events of Pentecost as they heard the Lord being praised in their own languages (v 11).

- **How is the Spirit already working to fulfill Jesus' commission in 1:8?**
The gift of tongues at Pentecost and the list of nations present to witness the event underscore the universal scope of the gospel. The "mighty works of God" (2:11) are already being communicated to those who come from nations that, to a 1st-century resident in the Roman Empire, would have represented the "end of the earth." It was no accident that God chose to send his Spirit to his people at this particular festival, when so many from different nations were gathered in Jerusalem.

NOTE: Two questions naturally arise from these verses, and are the source of great discussion among

Christians, and your group may ask you to give a view on them:

- *Are Christians filled with the Spirit when we come to faith, or is it a subsequent event?* The book of Acts and the rest of the New Testament make clear that Christians should not expect a later spiritual baptism after conversion. When believers come to faith in Christ, they also receive the Spirit. In fact, the Holy Spirit is the one who brings about the entire process of salvation. He convicts, he calls, and he regenerates (Titus 3:5). It's unbiblical to teach that one can be a true believer in Christ and yet be bereft of the Holy Spirit: "No one can say 'Jesus is Lord' except in the Holy Spirit" (1 Corinthians 12:3b). Today's Christians do not have to wait on a later gifting of the Holy Spirit in their experience of conversion. As Acts progresses, the expectation that followers of Christ also receive the Spirit upon conversion is seen as the norm.
- *Should believers today expect to speak in tongues?* Many good Christians today disagree over just this issue. One thing to recognize about Pentecost, however, is that it is a unique redemptive historical event. In fact, the experience of the way tongues were employed at Pentecost was different from how the gift of tongues was used in the early church. For instance, in 1 Corinthians 14, Paul corrects the abuse of tongues in the church at Corinth. He writes that a translation is required for the language because an untranslated language does nothing to edify the others present (1 Corinthians 14:6-19). The gift of tongues in Acts 2 did not require a translator; instead, those who were present heard the words in their own languages. This is because the purpose of the gift of tongues in Acts 2 was to enable the gospel to be heard by all those who had traveled to Jerusalem from foreign countries. The very purpose was to overcome any need for translation, not to require it!

4. In what different ways did people there respond to what they had seen and heard (v 11-13)?

- Amazement over being able to hear about God's works in their own language, from the mouths of Galileans.
- Perplexity over what it all meant.
- Mockery (v 13). (This accusation is ridiculous—have you ever met a drunk whose drinking enabled them to speak a language they'd never spoken before?!)

5. How did Peter explain...

- **what had just happened (v 16-21)?** Joel 2 prophesied that miraculous signs would accompany the pouring out of the Spirit in the "last days." According to the Old Testament, the "last days" were days of the new covenant and the new creation. Peter is essentially teaching the crowd that all of the Old Testament promises about the new creation have now been inaugurated by the work of Jesus Christ. The last days are now here, and the promised Spirit has now come.

- **who Jesus was (v 22-36)?**
  Peter described Jesus as…
  - a real man from a real place (v 22).
  - a man "attested to you by God" through his ability to perform wonders and signs that were witnessed by many (v 22)—Jesus was no mere man, and his miracles speak of his divine identity.
  - a man who was crucified (v 23), killed by lawless men who had been encouraged by the very people now listening to Peter. But note that Peter emphasizes God's sovereignty over this event. Jesus was delivered to death according to the predetermined plan of God. This does not mean that the men responsible for the crucifixion were without excuse; they were still guilty of their sin. The Bible holds both of these seemingly conflicting facts—God's sovereignty and man's responsibility—as harmonious truths.
  - the risen Lord. He was raised up from death by God, because death could not overpower him (v 24). This resurrection was witnessed (v 32); and as the risen Lord, Jesus is now seated at God's right hand (v 33). The one who was crucified is now the reigning, all-powerful Lord of all (v 36).

- **the right response to the resurrection of the Lord Jesus and the coming of the Spirit (v 37-40)?**
  First, repent. Sin demands repentance because sin is a violation of God's commandments. Mentally assenting to the wrongness of sin is not sufficient. That is not repentance. Feeling sad about the consequences of sin is not sufficient. That is mere regret. We demonstrate true repentance by a genuine hatred of sin, with a Spirit-empowered desire to never engage in that sin again, and a Spirit-driven determination to obey Jesus instead.

  Second, alongside repentance, Peter calls the crowd to be baptized. Baptism is an essential part of Christian discipleship and represents our forgiveness of sins. Baptism is not a prerequisite for salvation (the repentant thief on the cross was assured of his place in paradise, but was in no position to be baptized, Luke 23:40-43); the New Testament, however, has no category of a believer who does not choose to be baptized. Baptism is a necessary sign of obedience and discipleship. We do not need to be baptized to be saved; but if we are saved, then we will get baptized.

Explore More

- ***Read Luke 22:54-62 and John 21:15-19. In what sense is Peter himself an embodiment of the truths he is proclaiming about humanity, and about what Christ offers?***
  Consider how shocking it is that Peter was the preacher of this sermon. Peter had been a coward, even denying Jesus in the last moments of Jesus' earthly life, before realizing his sin and shedding tears over it (Luke 22:54-62). Yet he had been restored and commissioned by the risen Christ (John 21:15-19). The presence of Peter on the day of Pentecost is testament to the willingness of Christ to forgive even the worst of sinners.

---

6. **What was the result of Peter's sermon (v 41)?**
   Three thousand souls were added to the church that day. These words are evidence of the power of gospel proclamation through the Holy Spirit!

7. **What was this new-born church, full of 3,000 brand new Christians, like (v 42-47)?**
   - It was devoted to the apostles' teaching (v 42). This was a church gathered around, and under the authority of, the teaching of those men the Lord had appointed to see his ministry and witness his resurrection.
   - It was devoted to fellowship (v 42). This fellowship is not a superficial gathering around ham sandwiches and meringue pies. Fellowship in the church is based upon the common love that believers have for one another and their Lord. It was this love that motivated the early church to sell their possessions to meet the needs of those around them (v 44-45).
   - They dedicated themselves to the breaking of bread (v 42). The reference to "breaking of bread" refers to the celebration of the Lord's Supper, which the early church celebrated as a way of visually proclaiming and reminding one another of the gospel of Jesus Christ.
   - The church valued corporate prayer (v 42).
   - It was awestruck with the power and wonder of God (v 43). The things of God did not seem "normal" or everyday but wonderful and exciting.
   - This was a growing church (v 47). A church committed to gospel proclamation in reliance on the Spirit and to devotion to the word and each other will tend to be one that God is pleased to grow through conversions.

8. **How can your church today learn from the example of the early church here?**
   If any church is going to be an authentic church of the Lord Jesus Christ it will feature all four of these activities—the apostles' teaching (now

found in what we call the New Testament), fellowship, the Lord's Supper, and prayer. And it will be "devoted" to them. If any of these components are missing, there is a critical problem with the church's health.

So use your answers to question 7 to assess the spiritual health of your own church. Allow group members to make positive suggestions for how you might need to change to be more faithful to this scriptural picture of a healthy church; and be ready to feed back useful observations or critiques to your pastors—but endeavor to ensure this conversation remains constructive, rather than becoming overly negative.

9. **What was this man hoping for?**
   He was hoping for "alms" (v 3). As a lame man, he would have had no means of earning a living and would have been a huge drain on his family in mainly a subsistence culture. So the best he could do was to situate himself on a busy thoroughfare and hope for financial generosity.

- **In what sense was he disappointed, and in what sense was he satisfied?**
  He was disappointed in the sense that, as he looked at the apostles expectantly (v 5), Peter informed him that he had no silver or gold to give (v 6). The thing he needed would not be forthcoming. He was more than satisfied though, for Peter had something much more valuable to give. The man was being offered grace and healing by the power of the Holy Spirit. By verse 8, the man was able to stand, walk, and leap. He had received far more than he had expected!

10. **What similarities are there between this sermon and the response to it, and the previous one (2:14-41)?**
    - Most importantly, both sermons are all about Jesus.
    - Both lay out the foundational facts of Jesus' identity (2:23; 3:13), his death (2:23; 3:15) and the sinfulness it revealed (2:23; 3:13-15), and his triumphant resurrection (2:24, 36; 3:15), verified by witnesses (2:32; 3:15b).
    - Both call for repentance and offer forgiveness (2:38; 3:19).
    - Both make clear that Jesus is the climax and fulfilment of God's promises through his prophets (2:30-31; 3:18, 21-24).
    - Both at least hint that this offer of forgiveness upon repentance is for more people than the Jewish nation (2:39; 3:25-26).
    - As for the response: thousands repented and believed as a result of each sermon (2:41; 4:4).

11. **What differences do you notice?**
    NOTE: Remember, what is recorded in Acts is almost certainly Luke's summaries of longer "sermons," so any differences or "omissions" are not indications that these elements are unimportant.)
    - The Acts 2 sermon places more emphasis on the coming of the Spirit as the sign that the promised last days have arrived.

- The Acts 3 sermon contains more content on how God blesses those who repent:
    1. "Your sins [will] be blotted out" (v 19)—we must no longer bear our sins' penalty.
    2. "Times of refreshing [will] come" (v 20)—this likely refers to the hope of rest and renewal in the new creation.
    3. God will "send the Christ appointed for you" (v 20-21)—this refers to Christ's second coming, which those who have repented can look forward to, knowing he will be "for" rather than against them.
- In Acts 3, Peter makes no mention of baptism as he does in Acts 2. However, the rest of Acts shows that baptism was a normal part of the way someone became a Christian: the public sign of inner repentance and allegiance to Jesus as King. (See, for example, 8:34-38; 9:17-18.)
- As for the response: in Acts 2, we are only told of thousands repenting and believing. In Acts 4:1-4, we find around 2,000 converting (v 4); but the priests and their captain were "greatly annoyed" (v 2) and arrested and imprisoned Peter and John (v 3). This is the first note of serious opposition to and persecution of the church in Acts; it will not be the last.

12. How do Peter's two evangelistic sermons show us what faithful and effective witness will look like for us?

- It involves speaking, even when we face mockery or opposition.
- It must be centered on Christ—who he is, and what his death and resurrection mean.
- It must call for a response of repentance.
- It must set out what God in the gospel offers those who repent—namely, forgiveness of sins, the gift of the Spirit, and an eternal future with God.
- It must aim to call men and women to become disciples—members of churches.
- It can expect to prompt a response—sometimes positive, and sometimes negative. Faithful witness is not measured by the response to it but by its adherence to the gospel message.

3

Church Challenges

Acts 4:5 - 5:42

The Big Idea

The church overcomes both the external pressure to remain silent, and the internal temptation of living hypocritically, by remembering that Christ is the only way to be saved and that God is holy; and through prayer and fellowship.

Summary

These two chapters show us two great challenges to the early church (and to ours today). In Acts 4, Luke gives us our first glimpse of the division brewing between the people and the Jewish leaders. This division ultimately emerges from two things: (1) The apostles' preaching of the gospel, and (2) one specific aspect of the content of their preaching: namely, the resurrection from the dead.

Perhaps of most note in Acts 4 are two aspects of Peter and John's Spirit-enabled witness when they are dragged before the Sanhedrin (the court that had condemned the Lord as worthy of death, Luke 22:66 – 23:2):

- Acts 4:12: Peter makes it crystal clear that the gospel message is an exclusive one. There are not many paths to salvation and there are not many foundations upon which to build eternally. Instead, "there is salvation in no one else, for there is no other name under heaven given among men by which we must be saved." The doctrine of salvation is not an accessory to the Christian faith. Instead, salvation is the very heart of what Christ accomplished for those who respond to him in faith and repentance—and he is the only Savior.
- v 20: When the authorities order Peter and John "not to speak or teach at all in the name of Jesus" (v 18), they reply that, "we cannot but speak of what we have seen and heard." The way the disciples describe their mission as witnesses of Jesus in this verse is quite remarkable. They "cannot but speak" of Jesus. In other words, the gospel was not some theoretical philosophy. It was a message of salvation that had to be proclaimed.

The first challenge to the church in this passage is therefore external pressure to keep silent about the unique, exclusive nature of the gospel of the risen Christ. This challenge is to be met with prayer, and with a robust belief in God's sovereignty and ability to equip his people to boldly witness to the truth (4:23-31).

The second challenge is one of internal hypocrisy born out of half-hearted compromise. Acts 5:1-11 is one of the most remarkable and shocking narratives in all of the New Testament. God kills a husband and a wife for lying about their giving. Why? Because God is holy and must be worshiped as holy, rather than taking second place to selfish desires. God will not allow his church to become compromised by the hypocrisy of those who pretend to be devoted to him when in fact they are more devoted to themselves.

The third challenge, which this study covers very briefly, is really an extension of the first—continued, and increasing, opposition to the gospel. Once more, in 5:12-32, God's servants refuse to be silenced by pressure and threats, and indeed count it a privilege to suffer for the one who had suffered for them (v 41-42). When we, like they, trust in God's sovereignty and genuinely desire to see the kingdom of God advance, we will not resent God's trials in our lives, but we will even learn to rejoice in them.

Optional Extra

Have an extended time of prayer for the persecuted church. To help you, ask a group member to download some information and prayer points from an organization such as Open Doors (opendoors.org). Return at the end of your study to pray for such churches, that they would respond to pressure like the church did in Acts.

Guidance for Questions

1. **What are the greatest challenges your church faces?**
   Your group members may choose to focus on challenges posed by the culture, or by logistics, or by the particular make-up of your church membership, or socio-economic/demographic issues. There are no "wrong answers" at this stage—during the study you will reflect upon how the challenges faced in Acts 4 – 5 might manifest themselves today for your church membership. (See questions 8, 11, and 12.)

- **How do you think they can be overcome (if indeed they can)?**
  Do not dwell too long on this question, but equally, encourage positive answers.

2. **Read Luke 22:66 – 23:2, 10. Why would Peter and John have had every right to feel terrified in Acts 4:5-7?**
   This was the same court that had subjected Jesus to a show trial, and then insisted that he be sentenced to death. There would be no cause for the apostles to think that anything other than the same thing would happen to them now, if they maintained their public loyalty to Christ.

3. **What does Peter say about Jesus (v 8-12)?**
   The question of verse 7 presents an open door for the apostles to preach the gospel. And the apostles choose to walk through it.
   - First, Peter makes it clear that they do not preach or perform miracles in their own name or by their own power. Rather, they do all in the name of the Lord Jesus Christ. They are quick to point to the "means [by which] this man has been healed" (v 9).

- In verse 10, Peter addresses not only the Sanhedrin but all of Israel—"all of you." He claims with authority that the man was healed "by the name of Jesus Christ"—rejecting any attention that might be directed to him as the one who actually performed the miracle. Peter's primary concern is to point people to Jesus, the resurrected Lord.
- Peter continues his argument by claiming that Jesus is "the cornerstone" that Israel rejected (v 11—see Explore More for more on this)
- Peter makes it crystal clear that Jesus' offer is unique. There is salvation only in him, for his is the only name (i.e. he alone has the authority) that saves (v 12).

- **Why is he able to speak like this in such a setting (v 8)?**
  Peter is "filled with the Holy Spirit" before he begins his speech (v 8), again showing us how the Spirit emboldens and equips us for ministry.

Explore More

- ***Read Psalm 118:21-24. How does Peter's use of verse 22 in Acts 4:11 contain both a solemn warning and a wonderful promise?***
  The warning is that the religious leaders are rejecting the one who is central to all of God's plans. This is a truly dangerous position to be in. (See 1 Peter 2:7-8.) Further, the warning is that even the rejection of this cornerstone points to its true identity. Even the crucifixion of Jesus was forecast by the Scriptures.

  The promise is that God has clearly identified who is the cornerstone on which he builds—that there really is a way to be saved, and that is by being built into God's people, upon the "stone" of faith in Christ.

- ***Read Luke 20:9-18. How did Jesus himself use the same verse in a similar way?***
  Again, Jesus issues a warning and a promise. The warning is that those who reject him will be crushed—they choose to set themselves up against the rightful son and heir, and so they will lose their place in his vineyard (i.e. God's people living in God's place). To use the starker image of the cornerstone, they will be crushed by it.

  The promise is that those who build on Christ are part of God's eternal plans; they are those "others" (v 16) to whom the vineyard is given.

---

4. **What do Peter and John say about themselves (v 18-20)?**
   Aiming to calm the situation as quickly as possible, the authorities order Peter and John "not to speak or teach at all in the name of Jesus" (v 18). The apostles, however, point out that they are accountable to a higher authority: do they answer to God or men (v 19)? (To which question there is only one legitimate answer.)

So they must simply "speak of what they have seen and heard" (v 20). They are not at liberty to be quiet about Christ. They "cannot but speak" of Jesus. In other words, the gospel was not some theoretical philosophy. It was a message of salvation that had to be proclaimed.

5. How does the church respond to the threats of the religious and political elite?

Once the assembled believers heard about all that had happened to Peter and John, they did what many would not do—they prayed. The early church prayed without ceasing; it was a reflex to almost any circumstance. Prayer should be the Christian's natural first reaction to the testimony of God's power or a problem in God's world.

6. What do we learn here about prayer?

- *They begin by worshiping God for who he is*—they praise him as the matchless Creator (v 24). We, likewise, should praise God before we ask for what we need.
- *They quote Scripture* (v 25-26). It's worth noting that the early church used Scripture as a way to ignite their prayers. Rather than feeling the need to spontaneously "make up" their prayer, they prayed in response to God's word.
- *They recognize God's sovereign hand is in and over all things* (v 27-28). We must pray, therefore, just as the disciples prayed: mindful of and confident in the truth that God is truly sovereign. No area of our lives is beyond God's reach and sovereign plan.
- *They ask God not to spare them from further suffering but for faithfulness to preach Christ in that suffering* (v 29-30). They were praying, *Lord, in the face of opposition, don't let us weaken; don't let us compromise.* We too should pray more for faithfulness than we do for a change of circumstances.
- *Scripture-soaked prayers are answered.* The Spirit enabled them to do what they had asked—to proclaim the gospel (v 31).

7. Other than prayer, what else marked this church?

- *Visible fellowship* (v 32). This congregation was marked by its unity.
- *Mutual generosity* (v 32, 34-35). They knew the infinite value of Christ, so they loved one another freely by sharing their worldly possessions with one another.
- *Continued witness* (v 33). It might have been tempting to hold back and see how things played out, given that the church was now attracting the anger of the authorities; but instead, this church was (if anything) still more committed with their time, money, and possessions.

8. What would the challenges this church faced look like in your setting?

Think about what pressures you are under to compromise on the gospel either in the pulpit or in everyday witnessing. Think about whether there are legal pressures to compromise on how you live or what you say.

- **What would it look like for your church to respond to those challenges in the way this church did?**

  Think through, as practically and specifically as you can, what it would look like for you as a local church to follow the Jerusalem church in…
  - taking opportunities, even when being threatened, to point to the salvation that lies in Christ.
  - answering respectfully but boldly when told to be quiet.
  - praying together.
  - sharing together.

9. What is the challenge to the church in verses 1-11?

Take a brief moment to rehearse the narrative with your group, but do not allow yourself to become sidetracked by the whys and wherefores of what happened.

The challenge is that of Christians lying to one another in order to appear better than they really are. Ananias and Sapphira both claimed to be giving all that they had earned from the sale of their field; clearly they valued their money and their reputation more than they did their faith, their church, and the truth. This is hypocrisy: church members claim to be living in a committed, godly way while really serving themselves and pleasing themselves. This behavior is inspired by Satan (v 3) and involves lying not just to men, but to God (v 4).

10. How does this passage reveal to us God's view of hypocrisy?

Both Ananias (v 5) and Sapphira (v 10) do not survive. The stark truth is that God killed Ananias and Sapphira for their sin. That is how seriously God takes this kind of hypocritical approach to our holiness and our lives as part of his church.

- **What do you make of the severity of the punishment here?**

  We may well instinctively balk at it—but that is because we forget how holy God is, and how serious sin is: it is cosmic treason, a futile attempt to unseat God. We think one little lie is not deserving of Gods' wrath and the execution of it. But if we remember who God is, then we begin to grasp how serious sin is, and the shock becomes not that God did not spare Ananias and Sapphira, but that he sent his Son to die for sin so that there could be people who are spared, and so that there could be a church community of those who have been spared.

11. What forms might this challenge take in your church today?

To answer this question, think about what kind of Christian actions are particularly highly esteemed in your own church's culture. Then think about which of those actions it would be possible to pretend to do, or speak about doing, without actually doing them—or which could be done partially, in a way that looked very committed but actually held back or was self-serving. Those are likely to be the places where hypocrisy most easily flourishes.

- **How can you deal with it in a way that is serious but also gracious?**
  Some of us are predisposed to deal with sin ruthlessly and call it out in others, but to do so in a way that speaks too quickly, fails to listen well, and forgets to point to grace and move on in forgiveness. Others of us tend to go too far the other way, and never deal seriously with sin (never pointing it out, rebuking it, or reminding people of its seriousness) because we do not want to appear judgmental, or because we simply do not care about the seriousness of sin enough. You might like to read Matthew 7:3-5 and point out that we are to deal with our own sin before we challenge others on theirs; but that, equally, though humbly and acknowledging that we are not perfect, we are nevertheless to challenge others when needed (v 5).

- ***OPTIONAL (after reading verses 17-42): The Sadducees did not believe in angels. What is ironic about verses 17-21?!***
  The apostles are released by an angel, whom the Sadducees, their jailers, deny the existence of!

12. **What is challenging to us about the way that the apostles respond to what is done to them (v 41-42)?**
    (Notice that the seriousness of the opposition has increased; this time the apostles are whipped, v 40.)
    - Even with red-raw backs, they rejoice that they have been given the privilege of suffering for Christ (v 41). Not only do they not seek at all costs to avoid further suffering; they actually count it a blessing, for they are suffering in the cause of Christ's kingdom.
    - They "did not cease teaching and preaching that the Christ is Jesus" (v 42), which is the very thing they had been told not to do (v 40). They had prayed that threats would not prevent them from preaching truth (4:29)—and the Lord was pleased to answer that prayer in them.

    The challenge here is that all too often we prioritize avoiding pain or danger, even at the price of privatizing our faith. Far from seeing suffering for Christ as a privilege, we count it as a problem. Ask your group: what might it take for us to share the same view as the apostle here? You might point out that they had actually prayed that they would live like this—do we?

4

I See the Heavens Opened

Acts 6:1 - 7:60

The Big Idea

We are able to live and speak and even die for our faith when, like Stephen, we are filled with the Spirit, serve our church, speak the gospel, know how it will be received, and look forward to Christ welcoming us into his presence as we die in the faith.

Summary

Acts 6 introduces Stephen, the first martyr of the Christian church. 6:1-7 records a division that emerged in the early church and the establishment of a diaconate in order to resolve that problem (another challenge to the early church—the temptation either to fail to prioritize word ministry, or to completely neglect practical ministry). Stephen was among those first deacons. The second half of the chapter focuses on his evangelistic ministry, and the opposition that begins to mount against him.

This opposition leads to him being put on trial in chapter 7, accused of speaking against the temple and the Law. Stephen's defense reads like a history lesson, but it is an exercise in biblical theology—Stephen is retelling Israel's history in order to show how both the temple and the Law anticipated the person and the work of Christ; and to show how his opponents' rejection of him as Christ's messenger was nothing new—their forefathers had rejected the prophets (7:51-53).

His defense is unanswerable but provokes further rage, and Stephen becomes the first martyr of the Christian church, being stoned to death (7:54-60). But his last three statements show why he is willing and ready to die for Christ:

1. *He sees Jesus rising to welcome him to heaven (v 55-56).* Like a man rising up from his chair to greet a friend, Jesus rose to greet Stephen. In a sense, this is the visual declaration of what all Christians want to hear when they meet their Savior face to face: "Well done, good and faithful servant ... Enter into the joy of your master" (Matthew 25:21). It is also a reminder to Stephen that as Jesus is at the right hand of the God who is on the throne of the universe, nothing could happen to him without the consent of his loving and sovereign heavenly Father.
2. *He entrusts his spirit to Jesus (Acts 7:59).* The worst anyone can do to us is send us to Jesus. When we die with faith in the Lord Jesus, we will be received into his loving care.
3. *He prays for his persecutors (v 60)*, just as Jesus did (Luke 23:34). He is a true disciple, seeking to live as Jesus lived until he dies and is with him.

Stephen's martyrdom reminds us that the world hates the message of the gospel and will even resort to violence to see it squelched. But the church must not fear the persecution of the world. Our God reigns in heaven, and even if the world turns against us, we will, like Stephen, find Jesus standing in heaven, ready to receive us as we remain faithful to him. Knowing this will make us willing to serve the church like Stephen, to preach the gospel like him, and to die for Christ like him.

Optional Extra

See how much your group know about Christian martyrs throughout history by challenging them with a quiz. Print out pictures of various martyrs, e.g. Jim Elliot, William Tyndale, Dietrich Bonhoeffer. Read out short descriptions of how and why people died, and see if your group can guess who you are describing (e.g. "This person was killed in 1956 by indigenous people in Ecuador" = Jim Elliot).

Guidance for Questions

1. **What do you think it would take for you to be willing to die for your faith?**
   Encourage your group to be honest but also positive. Some will tend to take this question complacently as though every Christian would automatically be willing to die rather than deny Christ. Perhaps remind them that the apostle Peter would not have thought this! Equally, though, some would tend to assume they would not be able to stand firm in such a circumstance. But ordinary believers did (as in Acts 6 – 7), and still do worldwide today.

   We return to this subject in question 12, so you can leave this question hanging at this point, as the study will help build toward the answer.

2. **What was the challenge facing the church, and how was it resolved?**
   There seems to have been some discrimination, or at least perceived discrimination, in the way the church was caring for its widows. The "Hellenists," (i.e. the Greek-speaking Jews) were not receiving the same level of care as were the native Jerusalem widows (v 1).

   The apostles resolved the problem by asking the congregation to appoint "seven men of good repute, full of the Spirit and of wisdom" to care for the widows (v 3), which they duly did (v 5).

3. **How do the apostles prioritize word ministry without neglecting mercy ministry?**
   The apostles said, "It is not right that we should give up preaching the word of God to serve tables" (v 2). Later, in verse 4, the apostles again emphasize that they must wholly devote themselves "to prayer and to the ministry of the word." This response demonstrates that the apostles recognized that the most crucial aspect of any church is the faithful teaching and preaching of God's word and the ministry of prayer.

   Yet the apostles were not indifferent to the plight of the Hellenist widows. This is why they appointed these seven men: to ensure that the practical needs of these widows were met, and met in a way that was fair. These deacons were to free up the church's preachers and teachers from administrative concerns so that they could focus on the ministry of prayer and the word, while ensuring that those administrative and practical concerns were nevertheless being addressed. Neither ministry is optional for a healthy church, but the ministry of the word is utterly crucial.

Explore More

- ***Read 1 Timothy 3:1-7. What are the qualifications for being an "overseer"—that is, an elder or a pastor?***
  Encourage your group to put these qualifications into their own words. E.g. beyond any fair accusation; faithful in marriage; measured in thought; in control of their words and actions; morally upright; using their home to welcome others; able to teach the Scriptures; not becoming drunk, nor violent, nor pursuing wealth; able to raise his family in a godly way; a Christian of some longstanding; well-thought of in the community.
- ***Read 1 Timothy 3:8-13. What are the qualifications for being a deacon—serving the church through practical ministry as these seven men in Acts 6 did?***
  Upright in morals and bearing; honest in speech; not becoming drunk, nor pursuing wealth; clearly converted, and showing evidence of their suitability for the role; faithful in marriage; able to raise their family in a godly way.
- ***What differences do you see?***
  They are very similar—the clear key difference is that overseers must be "able to teach," since (as Acts 6 reminds us) this is their crucial role in serving and building the church.
- ***How do these lists underline the importance of both ministries?***
  Neither is a role to call someone to without careful thought; neither is for a new convert, or one who is not committed to a godly life. Our churches need those who serve them in word and practical ministries to be believers of integrity, faithfulness and devotion.
- ***How do they move us to pray for both our pastors/elders and our deacons (whether these are formal or informal roles)?***
  These lists, along with Acts 6, show us how much the church needs godly overseers and deacons who are serious about discharging their ministry faithfully. They need our prayers and our encouragement.

---

4. In what way is Stephen introduced to us here?
- He is one of the deacons chosen here (v 5).
- He is "a man full of faith and of the Holy Spirit."

5. **How does Luke continue to build a portrait of Stephen in these verses?**
   - He is full of grace and power, and (as with the apostles) God is pleased to work through him to authenticate his witness (v 8).
   - He is clearly a very able communicator, able to out-debate his opponents—a gift which is Spirit-given (v 9-10).
   - He has "the face of an angel" (v 15—see comment below question 6 in the Study Guide).

6. **Why did his opponents resort to underhand means?**
   Because they could not refute what Stephen was saying. True godliness often incites the world's fierce opposition. They could not defeat him in debate so they sought to silence him through prosecution.

7. **"Effective evangelism will lead to great fruit." Discuss, from this passage.**
   Let your group talk around this—there are different ways to think about it. You should aim to draw out the following thoughts:
   - If effectiveness or fruit is defined by number of conversions or number of church members, then this statement is false. Stephen's witness was clearly as bold and as faithful as Peter's back in Acts 2, but his speech (as we shall see) resulted in 3,000 fewer people repenting and believing—zero. Yet Christ was pleased with him and was waiting to greet him into heaven. So numbers is not how Jesus measures effective faithfulness in witness.
   - If by "fruit" we understand provoking a response or being seen by Christ as a good and faithful servant, then the statement is correct. This is the more biblical view. Faithful witness always produces a response, be it positive or negative. Effective evangelism leads to fruit, but that fruit is not necessarily the number of conversions.

- **What are the implications for our own everyday witness?**
  It is crucial that we grasp the lesson of Stephen's faithful witness here. If we do not, we shall be over-impressed by growing ministries/churches and not ask (or even care) whether the preaching is faithful; and in our own witness we shall seek to cut corners or duck controversial truths in order to "get results." Or we shall be over-discouraged by a lack of conversions through our own ministry, rather than seeking simply to be as faithful and compelling as possible.

8. **How does Stephen rebut these accusations?**

- **Speaking against Moses and the law (7:35-40, 52-53)**
  Luke shows that rather than speaking against Moses, Stephen was preaching against the cult of Moses, which ironically was staffed by those who denied what Moses had taught: namely, that there was coming a day when a greater Moses would come to redeem the people (7:37). By

preaching the word, Stephen countered the false understandings of his listeners with the way Scripture itself presents Moses: as a foreshadowing of the one who would come and lead his people in a greater exodus: the redemption of bondage to sin. Stephen demonstrates how Christ is greater than Moses was, and how the law was never intended to be the capstone of God's plan for his people. Stephen was upholding the true purpose of the law. The law was intended to demonstrate man's inability to live a life of obedience to the law (v 38-40), and so to point to our need for a savior. God's people themselves should have known this more than anyone, since they had received the law but had not kept it (v 53).

- **Speaking against God's temple (which was the place of God's presence among his people. Think about what Stephen is teaching his audience about God's presence in verses 2, 9, 30-33, 44-50.)**
    - God appeared to Abraham in Mesopotamia (modern-day Iraq, v 2)—outside the land and before the tabernacle or temple were ever constructed. God's presence is not confined to that place.
    - God was "with [Joseph]" in Egypt (v 9).
    - God visited Moses in the wilderness outside the promised land (v 30-33). That place was "holy" because God was present there.
    - This evidence leads to Stephen's conclusion in verse 48: "The Most High does not dwell in houses made by hands." The fact that God was never confined to the temple, and the fact that the story of God's presence develops across the pages of the Old Testament, demonstrate that the story of the temple was incomplete under the old covenant. True believers would have recognized that there would come a day when God would be with his people in a way that was even greater than under the old covenant.

9. **What picture does Stephen's unfolding of Old Testament history give us...**

- **of God?**

  He is a God who is present with his people; who makes promises to and for his people, and keeps them; who continually redeems and guides his people; who rules his people; who raises up those from among his people to be the means of his rescue and rule; and who does all this despite his people continually rejecting his word.

- **of God's people through the Old Testament?**

  They have rejected God's purposes and the people he has raised up for those purposes:
    - v 9-16: They rejected Joseph.
    - v 23-29, 39: They rejected Moses.
    - v 52-53: They resisted the Holy Spirit by refusing to listen to the prophets.

10. **What is Stephen's conclusion about his listeners, and what is their conclusion about him (v 51-58)?**
In verses 51-53, Stephen becomes the prosecutor in this court scene and charges his audience with the ultimate crime: "You stiff-necked people, uncircumcised in heart and ears, you always resist the Holy Spirit" (v 51). Stephen's scathing indictment has the ring of an Old Testament prophet. The people of Israel are now rejecting Jesus, through rejecting his messenger Stephen.

Their conclusion about him is that he is deserving of death. They are enraged (v 54), grinding their teeth at him (this is animalistic; it demonstrates raw, absolute anger or pain). Upon hearing Stephen's declaration that he has seen a vision of Jesus at the right hand of Yahweh, they "rushed together at him" (v 57).

11. **What do Stephen's last three utterances teach us about dying well (v 55-60)?**
    - "Behold, I see the heavens opened, and the Son of Man standing at the right hand of God" (v 56). Like a man rising up from his chair to greet a friend, Jesus rose to greet Stephen. In a sense, this is the visual enactment of what all Christians want to hear when they meet their Savior face to face: "Well done, good and faithful servant ... Enter into the joy of your master" (Matthew 25:21). When we die full of faith, we die a good death, and are welcomed by our Lord the other side of it.
    - "Lord Jesus, receive my spirit" (Acts 7:59). Just as the Lord himself entrusted his spirit to his Father as he died (Luke 23:46), so his followers can too. The worst anyone can do to us is send us to Jesus. When we die with faith in the Lord Jesus, we will be received into the loving care of that Lord Jesus.
    - "And falling to his knees he cried out with a loud voice, 'Lord, do not hold this sin against them'" (Acts 7:60). This prayer reflects Jesus' own intercession for his persecutors in Luke 23:34: "Father, forgive them, for they know not what they do." This parallel between Stephen and Jesus marks Stephen as a true disciple. He is following in the footsteps of his Savior. Even in death, God is conforming Stephen into the image of Christ, as he promises to do for all his children (Romans 8:29).

12. **What did Stephen know that enabled him to live as he did and die as he did?**
Fundamentally, he knew the gospel. He knew that God keeps his promises to his people; he knew that Christ had called him to be a witness to him; he knew that, though a deacon and not an "overseer" of the church, he was yet called to boldly proclaim Christ; he knew that beyond death Christ was waiting for him in glory, ready to welcome him in.

- **What would it take for you to be willing to live like that, and (if called to) to die like that?**
We simply need to know and truly believe what Stephen did. And if we feel that we do not or might not, then we need to ask the Spirit to work in us. Stephen lived and died as he did because he was full of the Spirit (6:5, 10; 7:55). It is as the Spirit works in us that we are enabled to become bold, faithful ministers and witnesses, as Stephen was.

5

Beyond Jerusalem

Acts 8:1-40

The Big Idea

What look like setbacks—including persecution and false conversion—can be used by God to grow his kingdom. So as his people, we must keep sharing Christ with everyone we can, asking God to use us to build his church.

Summary

The open persecution of the church in Jerusalem forced the church to scatter throughout the regions of Judea and Samaria (8:1). This flight of Christians from Jerusalem is very significant in terms of redemption history. Acts 8 shows that Jerusalem is no longer the center of what God is doing in his world, nor is it the place where God is most present in his world—his "holy temple" is now the gathered local church, a "dwelling place [of] God by the Spirit" (Ephesians 2:21-22).

In fact, we see in this scattering of Christians to Judea and Samaria the fulfillment of Christ's purposes for his church. Jesus had said the church would be his "witnesses in Jerusalem and in all Judea and Samaria, and to the end of the earth" (Acts 1:8). And so the persecution of the church only served God's purposes for the expansion of his kingdom and the advance of the gospel.

Acts 8:5 turns our attention to one of those scattered in particular: Philip. Philip was a Jewish Christian who, along with Stephen, had been appointed to serve as one of the seven deacons in 6:1-6. Philip's actions in Acts 8, however, do not derive from his role as deacon, but instead are a further outworking of the theological upheaval happening in the hearts and minds of Jewish Christians. If he had been following the logic of traditional Jewish theology, Philip would have avoided Samaria at all costs. Samaria was considered unclean because the people had intermarried with Gentiles and had changed their worship practices. Yet Philip went to Samaria and "proclaimed to them the Christ" (Acts 8:5)—and "the crowds with one accord paid attention to what was being said" (v 6). This was a sure sign that the new covenant would include people from all nations. The gospel was breaking beyond the boundaries of Jerusalem and moving even to the unclean Samaritans.

The next part of Acts 8 shows how *not* to respond to the gospel—or perhaps more specifically, it shows us a false conversion to Christ. Simon the Sorcerer professed faith and was baptized; but his offer of money to the apostles in payment for the ability to "give" the Spirit to people shows that he was more concerned with his own reputation and power than he was with Christ's. His heart, Peter says, was not right, and repentance (rather than money) was what he needed to offer (v 22). Simon wanted the benefits of the gospel but would not truly submit his life to King Jesus.

The second half of Acts 8 shows us a genuine picture of conversion in the person of the Ethiopian eunuch. God's Spirit directs Philip to the eunuch's chariot as he returns to Ethiopia from Jerusalem. He is reading Isaiah, but cannot understand who the prophet is speaking of—Philip uses that passage to proclaim Jesus to him.

Having just come from Jerusalem where, as a eunuch, this man would have been barred from full access to the temple, now he discovers that he can be included in the very kingdom of God. The eunuch's baptism marks his formal and full identification with God's people (v 38). Once again, Luke is showing his readers that the gospel is breaking out of the boundaries of Israel.

There are several lessons for the church today:

- We should not allow our own prejudices to steer us away from witnessing to those who seem unlikely to come to faith. In fact, the most apparently rocky soil may prove the most fertile.
- False converts should never deter us from the mission to preach the good news.
- The core of the good news is the person and work of Jesus Christ. He is the one we must talk about most of all, and without fail.

Optional Extra

Host a mock auction. Give each member a budget (you could give them a stack of notes from a game like Monopoly); then auction off a range of items—from boring but useful household articles to exciting once-in-a-lifetime experiences. Who will "spend" their money on what? Finish with something that is beyond monetary value—make the point that there are some things that money simply cannot buy, as Simon the Sorcerer discovers.

Guidance for Questions

1. **Have you ever experienced a terrible situation from which great good resulted?**

- **Did that experience cause you to look differently at life in any way? How?**
  Prepare your own answer to this question before the group meet (if you do not have one from your own life, seek to find one from someone you know, or one you have read about). Encourage your group to share their stories in a concise way. The sub-question is as important as the first part. You could return to this question after question 2, 3 or 5, and answer it in terms of the experience of the early church.

2. **What state did the church seem to be in by the end of verse 3?**
   Not good. The open persecution of the church in Jerusalem forced the believers to scatter throughout Judea and Samaria (v 1). Those who remained mourned Stephen (v 2). Saul ravaged the church, systematically moving from house to house to imprison every believer he could find (v 3). Things were looking very bleak.

- **What state did the church seem to be in by the end of verse 8?**
  Very good. The scattering of the believers had brought the gospel to Samaria (v 5), and the people there "paid attention," so that there was "much joy" over the sound and signs of the gospel (v 8). Point out to your group that Jesus' commission in 1:8 was being fulfilled.

  - ***OPTIONAL: What was it that turned the situation from bleak to positive?***
    Verse 4: The scattered believers "went about preaching the word." The Christians could have seen the scattering as a disaster; instead they appear to have viewed it as an opportunity to serve and proclaim Christ.

3. **Read John 4:7-9. How does this context make the growth of the church in Samaria all the more wonderful?**
   Jews and Samaritans did not speak or have dealings with one another. That was how intense the mutual hatred was. Jews considered Samaria unclean because the people had intermarried with Gentiles. In fact, the Jews used the designation "Samaritan" as an insult (John 8:48). It was not by accident that the Lord used a Samaritan as the "hero" of his parable about defining who our neighbor is (Luke 10:25-37). Samaria was rocky, unlikely ground for planting a church. Yet it was here that Philip preached, and here that a new church was born as the word was received with joy (Acts 8:8).

4. **What was Simon's status before Philip arrived?**
   Verses 9-11: He was known throughout the city as a sorcerer with great power. In fact, "from the least to the greatest," the people of Samaria would say "This man is the power of God that is called Great" (v 10). He held the attention of the city (v 11).

- **What did Simon desire after Philip and the apostles had arrived (v 18-20)?**
  He was so impressed by the power of the apostles that he offered to pay the apostles money to receive the Spirit in order that he would possess the abilities they did (v 18-19). He wanted to "obtain the gift"—the power—that they had (v 20).

- **What did Peter identify as Simon's problem (v 21-23)?**
  Peter revealed the true state of Simon's heart. He wanted to enjoy and employ the power of the gospel, but his heart was not right—he was not truly loving and seeking to serve Christ as his King. Peter drives this point home when he denounces Simon's action as "wickedness," and claims that he is in the "gall of bitterness" and "bond of iniquity" (v 23). Simon's desire for the Spirit's power was in order to serve himself (presumably by restoring himself to his previous position of power and influence among the people), rather than to work for the good of the church.

Explore More

- ***If you had been there at the end of verse 13, what would you have made of Simon?***
  Simon had believed, had been baptized, and had joined Philip. You and I would have seen a new, keen, committed Christian, engaged in ministry.

- ***Read Matthew 7:21-23; 13:18-23 and James 2:14-19. What do Jesus and James say are the real signs of a truly converted heart?***
  Genuine conversion leads to a genuine change of life and a daily walk in repentance. As Jesus taught, "Not everyone who says to me, 'Lord, Lord,' will enter the kingdom of heaven, but the one who does the will of my Father who is in heaven" (Matthew 7:21). As James reminds us, even the demons believe (James 2:19). That belief is useless—what matters is having a repentant faith that shows itself in the way a person lives.

---

5. **What should the spread of the church into Samaria teach your church today?**
   - Our sovereign God acts in ways that confound the wisdom of the world. The more the world opposes the church, the more the Lord preserves and protects the gospel. What we see as setbacks, the Lord uses for advance; where we see a detour from the obvious route, the Lord has so often plotted out a path to the growth of his people and the glory of his Son. Does your church have this positive view of difficulties, hardships, and setbacks?
   - If Samaritans would listen to the gospel and respond positively, and if they would come into the fledgling church, then anyone can. Are there people groups or communities whom your church makes no

effort to reach because their conversion seems so unlikely?

6. **How should the example of Simon warn us as believers today?**

   Simon should prompt us to consider the state of our own belief in Jesus. Is it intellectual or is it true heart belief? Does it issue forth in repentance and change (albeit sometimes frustratingly slowly as we do battle with our sin)? Do we want the benefits God offers in the gospel, or do we want to know the God of the gospel? Peter urged Simon to believe in a way that affected his whole life—to exhibit a faith and repentance in which the head, heart, and soul are all connected. We should be warned to take a careful look at ourselves to discern what the nature of our "belief" is too. It is possible to profess faith and be baptized, and yet have a heart that is not right with God.

7. **What does Luke tell us about the man in the chariot (v 27-28)?**
   - He was an Ethiopian. Romans considered Ethiopia the "edge of the world"—a place with little reputation.
   - He was a eunuch. (See note on this in Study Guide, page 34.)
   - He was a "court official"—he was literate.
   - He had come to Jerusalem to worship.
   - He was clearly drawn to the God of Israel (though again, see note in Study Guide).
   - He was reading the prophet Isaiah.

8. **What role in this unlikely conversion is played by...**

- **the word of God?**

  It was reading the prophet Isaiah which had grasped the attention, and prompted the questions, of this man. We should note the centrality of the word of God in this encounter. Even as the Spirit supernaturally guides Philip to this conversation with the Ethiopian, the Lord uses the word of God and the ministry of Philip as the mechanism of the Ethiopian's conversion. Our temptation is to wish for supernatural displays of power. But God delights in using his written word to convert the lost and expand his kingdom.

- **a servant of God?**

  In the ancient world reading was done aloud. As Philip approached the chariot, he would have heard the eunuch reading the prophet—so he asked, "Do you understand what you are reading?" (v 30). The Ethiopian admits he needs someone to guide him and help him understand the message of Isaiah (v 31). So Philip tells him how Isaiah was pointing toward the person and work of Jesus Christ (v 35). This passage provides a glorious picture of how God uses his people and his word in tandem to advance the gospel throughout the world.

9. **What does this episode teach us about the Old Testament?**

   The Old Testament, as Jesus himself said, all points toward the identity, suffering, and glory of Christ (Luke 24:27). So every passage in the Old Testament speaks to us of Jesus, as Philip showed here. As the great Victorian preacher C.H. Spurgeon put it, we are to read a text and then make a beeline for the cross.

10. **What suggests that the eunuch's conversion was genuine (v 36-39)?**
First, he wants to be baptized (v 36-38). Having just come from Jerusalem where he has been barred from full access to the temple, now the eunuch discovers that he can be included in the very kingdom of God. The eunuch's baptism marks his formal and full identification with God's people (v 38).
Second, he rejoices (v 39), even after the Spirit has taken Philip away. His evangelist may have gone, but his Savior has not—and so he is full of joy. Simon, remember, has been baptized too—but he was full of envy and ambition, rather than the joy that is produced by real conversion (v 8).

11. **What reasons could Philip have come up with for not preaching the gospel at various points in this chapter?**
    - Verse 5: He had been forced to leave his home, city, and church. Christians were being imprisoned. Philip could very easily have decided it was wiser to keep quiet.
    - Verse 24: Having seen Simon, this powerful popular figure, apparently converted through his ministry, it must have been of great disappointment to Philip to see that Simon was, in fact, not right with the Lord in his heart. (Notice he does not, even in verse 24, really repent—he merely asks that the negative consequences of his sin would not catch up with him). It would have been easy to have given up at this point.
    - Verse 26: The Spirit required Philip to take an arduous journey without telling him its purpose. Staying home must have seemed much more attractive than going.

- **What would he not have experienced if he had given up at each of those points?**
Be sure that God would still have called his people to place their faith in him. But Philip had the privilege of seeing the gospel take root in Samaria... and of seeing it spread through the villages in Samaria... and of witnessing to and baptizing the Ethiopian eunuch. His willingness to go where the Spirit led him, and to see setbacks as opportunities to keep proclaiming Christ (rather than excuses not to), meant that he had the privilege of being a way in which the Lord worked to spread his gospel, win his people, and build his church. Note that the Getting Personal section on page 36 encourages your group members to think about their own witness.

12. **How should this chapter lead us to think about the possibility of**

Christians being persecuted in our culture or country?

Persecution may well be coming to the West—it may have already arrived in your particular location to some extent. We must not see this as a disaster or as something out of the ordinary—it is the normal experience of the church through the ages, including the church in Acts. And we should see such persecution as an opportunity—to show more clearly the surpassing worth of knowing Christ, and to share him with others—be that on our street, or in prison, or wherever we find ourselves. The Lord can and does work through the enmity of his people's opponents to grow his people.

6

The Most Unlikely Conversion

Acts 9:1-43

The Big Idea

God can bring anyone to faith and use anyone to build his church—we should respond by faithfully, boldly witnessing to and caring for others, trusting in God's power and purposes.

Summary

Acts 7 and 8 fleetingly introduced us to one of the most important figures in the New Testament: Saul, better known to us as the apostle Paul. In 7:58, the witnesses of Stephen's persecution laid their robes at Saul's feet as a sign of his authority over and agreement with the proceedings. Then 8:3 revealed that Saul had one overwhelming mission in life: to stamp out the spread of the gospel. But the grace of God would soon bring that reign of terror to an end. Acts 9 returns to Saul's story.

We meet Saul on the road to Damascus, purposing to arrest and imprison any believers he finds there. He begins his journey in strong defiance of the gospel, but he enters Damascus guided by the hands of others, having lost his sight. Saul had experienced the blinding light of Christ and was apprehended by the gospel (v 3-5). Instead of Saul laying hold of Christians, Jesus Christ had laid hold of him.

Saul's conversion may well shock us, but this is an indicator that we have not grasped the wonder of God's sovereign grace. We ought to expect the unexpected from God. God ransomed one of the most unlikely men—a persecutor of the church, no less—to be a frontrunner for his church. Saul has been chosen to bring the gospel to the Gentiles, and to suffer in so doing (Acts 9:15-16)—and he quickly learns that ministry will involve persecution (v 23-25).

Notice, too, the lessons for discipleship in the examples of Ananias and Barnabas. Ananias is told by the Lord to reveal himself as a believer to a man he knows as a persecutor of Christians (v 10-14). Yet, with the Lord graciously revealing that he has chosen Saul to serve him, Ananias goes to Saul and calls him "brother" (v 17). Barnabas, too, is willing to love and forgive the man who had hurt his brothers and sisters (v 27).

The study finishes by briefly looking at the second half of the chapter, in which Jesus uses his power to work through Peter to heal a lame man and raise a woman from the dead, causing many to believe in him (9:32-42). The resurrection of Tabitha teaches us several things:

1. Christ is powerful—even over death.
2. We all anticipate a greater resurrection to come.
3. The kingdom into which we have been saved is one of life, without death.

Optional Extra

As everyone gathers at the start of your time together, blindfold several volunteers so that they cannot see at all. After ten minutes or so, let them take their blindfolds off. Ask them how they felt, and in what ways they had to trust those who could see. Lead into a discussion of Saul's experience—the Lord humbled this proud man by blinding him: a sign of how low we must go in order to be ready to repent and come under Jesus' lordship. Further, in order to be willing to go and visit Saul—that sworn enemy of the church—Ananias had to be willing to trust the Lord's word about something he had not seen—Saul's Damascus road experience.

Guidance for Questions

1. **Of the people you know, who do you consider least likely to become a Christian? Why?**

   This may be a celebrity or politician, but encourage your group to consider those they know who live near them, or are in their families or workplaces.

2. **Why was Saul such an unlikely convert to Christianity? (v 1-2; see also 7:58 – 8:3.)**

   In 7:58, Luke writes that those who stoned Stephen to death laid their robes at Saul's feet; it was a sign of his authority over and agreement with the proceedings. Saul may not have thrown stones at Stephen, but he was certainly morally culpable. In many respects, he could even be seen as one of the leaders in instigating Stephen's martyrdom. Then 8:3 reveals that Saul had one overwhelming mission in life: to stamp out the spread of the gospel. He was utterly determined to end Christianity.

3. How does Jesus describe the relationship between Saul and himself (Acts 9:4-5)?

Saul is persecuting him. Can you imagine how Saul felt at that moment? The Lord of the people he had been imprisoning and even killing was, in fact, real; and was, in fact, infinitely powerful.

- **What does this tell us about the relationship between Jesus and his church?**

  To persecute Christ's people is to persecute Christ himself. That is how closely Jesus identifies with his people, and how much he cares about his people. Just as the attack on 9/11 was an attack on America, despite being targeted at only two locations in two cities, so any attack upon a believer is viewed by the Lord as being an attack on him.

4. What is impressive about Ananias' obedience here?

To him, it must have seemed as if God were sending him to seek out persecution, imprisonment, and even death by asking him to go to see Saul and reveal himself to be a Christian. Yet the Lord gave a simple and direct imperative: "Go!" And Ananias chose to obey, entering the dwelling of his new brother in Christ (v 17). He took a risk, based only on God's word to him (v 15-16). He chose to trust God instead of his view of the situation. This is, of course, far easier said than done.

5. What does the Lord reveal about his plans for Saul (v 15-16)?

First, God had chosen Saul to "carry my name before the Gentiles and kings and the children of Israel" (v 15). God intended to use this new convert to spread the gospel throughout the nations. And as the rest of the New Testament affirms, this is exactly what Saul did. Second, the Lord also shared with Ananias that Saul's mission would not be easy: "I will show him how much he must suffer for the sake of my name" (v 16). Saul would later find joy in suffering for the sake of Christ; rather than continuing as one who persecuted the church, Saul would himself endure persecution for the church, ultimately culminating in his martyrdom in Rome.

6. Why were the residents of Damascus right to be "amazed" (v 21)?

Because Saul, who had intended to hunt for Christians in the synagogues of Damascus, now entered the synagogues preaching Christian truth. "Jesus," he proclaimed, "is the Son of God" (v 20). (Notice that Saul did not wait; he immediately began to show his fellow Jews that Jesus Christ was the Messiah of the Old Testament.)

Saul's original mission to persecute Christians was so well known that "all who heard him" were amazed and wondered if Saul, the man now preaching Christ in the synagogue, was the same Saul who had come to Damascus to kidnap

Christians (v 21). The person who would have been voted least likely to become a Christian by his rabbinical school now stood as a vocal proponent of Jesus Christ. Mistaken identity seemed a more likely explanation than the truth!

Explore More

- ***Read Philippians 3:4-11 and 2 Corinthians 11:22-29. What was life like for Saul/Paul before he was converted, and after?***

  Before: Saul had every advantage of birth, upbringing, and religious training and position. Philippians 3:4-6 is, in terms of 1st-century Israel, a very impressive résumé. He would have been immensely respected.

  After: 2 Corinthians 11:22-29 reminds us what Saul/Paul's life was actually like as the apostle to the Gentiles. Still a Hebrew, but now a servant of Christ (v 22-23), he was imprisoned, beaten, and sometimes almost killed. He was stoned, shipwrecked, in danger, and hungry. And he bore the burden of his ministry in his concern for the Christian walk of those brothers and sisters in the churches he had planted.

- ***How do his words in Philippians show that it was worth giving up all that he had in order to suffer all that he endured?***

  "For the sake of Christ" Paul "counted as loss" all he had once had (v 7). The "surpassing worth of knowing Christ Jesus [his] Lord" meant any loss of safety, reputation, or position were worth it (v 8). When we live for and suffer for Christ, whatever we give up cannot possibly compare with the joy of knowing him as our Lord and Savior, and the anticipation of one day rising to live with him (v 11).

---

7. How should God's sovereign power in converting people encourage us in our own prayers and witness?

Very simply, we ought to keep praying for the lost, and keep speaking gospel truth to the lost. Luke reminds us throughout Acts that there is no one beyond God's reach, which is a lesson we continually need to be taught. Ask your group: If the Lord could convert Saul—and if the Lord could convert you—then what will stop you living as though he can reach those around you, meaning that you lose out on the privilege of being the way he reaches them? Considering God's sovereign power in evangelism will keep us prayerful and keep us witnessing.

8. How does Paul begin to be shown this here?

The bewilderment of the Jewish leaders erupted into a murderous plot—a further ironic twist in Saul's conversion story (v 23). The persecutor turned preacher was now the persecuted. Saul found out about the plot, however, and escaped from Damascus with the help of the church. Saul was let down in a basket from the city walls to hide from the Jewish leaders who wanted to take his life. Saul, a man who once held a place of such dignity that he would not get his hands dirty in the stoning of Stephen, now experienced a humiliating rescue operation. From the beginning, his ministry involved difficulty, persecution, and attempts on his life.

9. **What are the similarities between the events of 9:36-43 and Luke 8:40-56?**
   - A female had died, and her friends/ family begged Peter/Jesus for help.
   - The mourning had begun.
   - The room was cleared.
   - Both Dorcas and Jairus' daughter were raised through a word of command.
   - Both were raised by the power of Jesus (in Luke 8, he simply spoke; in Acts 9, Peter prays and then speaks).

- **What are the similarities and differences between the events of Acts 9:36-43 and what Paul writes in 1 Corinthians 15:51-53?**

  One day, just as Christ through Peter called Dorcas out of her grave, so Christ will in person call all his people out of the grave. We shall all be given our resurrection bodies and will "put on immortality" (1 Corinthians 15:54)—unlike Dorcas here, we shall experience a resurrection to life without any prospect of facing the grave again.

10. **What was the outcome both of Saul's conversion and ministry (v 31), and Peter's signs and ministry (v 35, 42)?**
    - v 31: The church was at peace and was built up, and multiplied.
    - v 35: The church grew as people turned to the Lord.
    - v 42: Many believed in the Lord.

11. **How are lives changed in Acts 9, and by what means?**
    - Saul's life is changed by the direct involvement of Jesus, speaking his word to him; and then through the courageous ministry of Ananias.
    - Aeneas' and Dorcas' lives are changed through the miraculous ministry of the apostle Peter.
    - Do not miss the fact that countless lives are changed through the teaching ministry of both Saul and Peter. Those who are not named, but who hear the gospel and believe, also have their lives changed as they pass from death to life.

12. **What have we learned about true discipleship from...**
    - **Saul?**

      It involves speaking of Christ, even when that brings hardship. It also requires a complete break from what we once held most dear: the things of this world.

    - **Ananias?**

      It involves risky and potentially very costly obedience. When God speaks to us in his word, we are to obey him, no matter what the risks involved are. As we do this, we find ourselves being part of the way God works out his purposes for his people in his world.

- **Barnabas?**
  It involves being willing to love those who once sought to hurt us; and being open to what the Lord might have done, or be doing, in the most unlikely of people. Christians should be the quickest to extend a hand of friendship and forgiveness.

7

To the Gentiles

Acts 10:1 - 11:30

The Big Idea

God made clear that salvation in Christ is available to Gentiles—to all people. Grasping this leads to churches that are known for their loyalty to Christ, witness to non-Christians, and generosity toward other believers.

Summary

The beginning of chapter 10 introduces us to Cornelius, a centurion in the Italian Cohort of the Roman army, a prestigious, elite unit (since it was Italian). He was also a God-fearer—a non-Jew who had been drawn to worship the God of Israel and acknowledge him as the one true living God.

The real drama begins with two visions: an angel visits Cornelius to tell him to send for a man named Peter, and he is obedient (v 3-8); and Peter receives a vision in verses 9-16, in which the Lord informs him that there is no clean/unclean distinction in what his people may eat. Peter understands this to mean that the Lord is no longer calling his people to remain distinct from the Gentiles, as he had Old Testament Israel, but rather that they are now to offer the gospel to the Gentiles (v 27-28, 34-36, 43). Therefore, he travels to Cornelius' house with Cornelius' servants. Peter is willing to obey his Lord even when that moves him a long way beyond his comfort zone.

When Peter preaches Christ to the assembled household (v 36-43), the Spirit leads them to turn to Christ and speak in tongues (v 44-46). Peter therefore baptizes them (v 47-48).

Some take these events as evidence that when someone receives the Holy

Spirit, they should also speak in tongues. But that reading of the text misses the point of the passage by failing to read it in its context. This entire chapter has focused, not on the gift of tongues, but on the inclusion of the Gentiles in the Christian community. The coming of the Spirit on the Gentiles and their speaking in tongues is meant to remind us of Acts 2. It demonstrates that the same Spirit has fallen on both Jews and Gentiles. If these two groups share one Spirit, then they are one body—united by faith in Christ and all members of his church. This was, in effect, Pentecost for the Gentiles.

In Acts 11, Peter defends his actions to the believers in Jerusalem, some of whom are critical (v 2-3). It is important to realize that this was no mere ugly prejudice, but motivated by a desire for holiness and distinctiveness in God's people. Their aversion, while wrong, was not wrongly motivated. When Peter explains what happened and the evidence that it was Spirit-led, they praise God (v 18). This is key—the Jerusalem church is recognizing that Gentiles can become full members of the covenant community.

The church in Antioch mirrors the work of the Spirit through Peter, witnessing to Gentiles ("Hellenists") and to Jews (v 19-20) with great conversion fruit (v 21). The church there becomes known for its witness (v 19-21), its loyalty to Christ (v 26—here is the first time the believers are known as "Christians") and for its generous giving to the Jewish church in Jerusalem (v 29), displaying the unity between churches across the ethnic boundaries. Truly, the Gentiles had become full members of Christ's church.

Optional Extra

If you normally serve refreshments to your group, try switching appetizing snacks to something your group will think looks and tastes disgusting, e.g. edible dried insects or pickles with ice cream. How do they feel? Will your group be brave enough to try it? Do they trust you? During the study, make the point that Peter's surprise and disgust at being asked to eat unclean food had much deeper religious and cultural roots.

Guidance for Questions

1. **What is your church's reputation among other like-minded churches? If they had to sum up your church in three words or phrases, what would they be, do you think?** Note that this question is not about your church's reputation with your local community, but with churches that view the authority of the Bible in the same way yours does, and that know of your church. You'll return to this idea in question 12.

2. **What do we learn about Cornelius in verses 1-2?**
   - v 1: He was a centurion in the Italian Cohort of the Roman army. The Italian Cohort's officers were among the elite, and Cornelius' name is distinctly Roman, suggesting that he himself was Italian, which would place him in the higher social classes of Rome.

- v 2: He was a God-fearer. This term refers to Gentiles who had been drawn to the worship of the God of Israel and had come to acknowledge Yahweh as the one true and living God. Gentile God-fearers could not become Jews in any specific sense. Judaism in the 1st-century was not a missionary religion. It would have been virtually impossible for a Roman officer of the Italian Cohort to become Jewish. Nevertheless, he had a heart for God and was seeking to please him, as was his whole household; and so he supported the Jewish people financially.

3. **Trace the path of events that leads to Peter visiting Cornelius in Caesarea.**

   Encourage your group to give concise descriptions for each mini-section below. The aim is simply to understand the narrative, before the next questions consider its significance.

- **v 3-8**
  Cornelius sees and hears an angel of the Lord in a vision. The sight of this angel, who speaks to Cornelius by name, understandably terrifies him (v 4). The angel informs Cornelius that God accepts his prayers and alms as a memorial, and instructs Cornelius to send some men to locate Simon Peter, giving details of where in Joppa he can be found (v 5-6). Cornelius obeys by commanding his men to go get Peter, and not to return without him (v 7-8).

- **v 9-16**
  Peter goes out on the rooftop of his host's house to pray. While Peter is praying, he becomes hungry (v 10). He falls into a trance and sees the sky opening up and all kinds of animals displayed on a great descending sheet (v 11-12). He hears a voice which he recognizes as God's (v 13). The voice commands Peter to rise, kill, and eat the animals. Peter says he will not eat anything unclean, but the Lord tells Peter he has no right to call unholy what God has cleaned (v 15). The sequence happens three times before the vision stops (v 16).

- **v 17-20**
  Peter is perplexed, but has little time to think because Cornelius' men arrive (v 17-18). The Spirit tells Peter to go with them (v 19-20).

- **v 21-23**
  The men inform Peter of the reason for their journey, and he invites them in, before accompanying them to Cornelius' house the next day.

- **v 24-29**
  Cornelius, who has been waiting for his men to return with Peter, calls together his relatives and close friends (v 24). Believing Peter to be a man of high esteem and worthy of worship, he falls at the apostle's feet. Peter, as we've seen time and again through the book of Acts, refuses to accept any exaltation of himself (v 26), and instead begins to proclaim to those who have gathered there the truth of

the only one who is worthy of worship (v 28-29). Peter points out that Jews do not visit Gentiles (v 28), but also reveals that he has understood the correlation between the acceptability of the animals in his vision, and the status of the people he is standing before—which is why he is standing in this Gentile's house (v 29).

- **v 30-33**
  Cornelius recounts the angelic vision he saw, and indicates that they are ready to listen to whatever Peter's God-given message is.

Explore More

- ***Based on what Peter says to God, what kinds of animals did the sheets in Peter's vision clearly contain (v 12-14)?***
  Literally "all kinds," including those that Peter viewed as "common or unclean."
- ***Read Leviticus 11:1-47. Why is Peter's response to being told, "kill and eat" understandable?***
  Old Testament dietary laws forbade the eating of cloven-hoofed animals, scavengers, and pigs. Peter seems to think the Lord is putting his orthodoxy to the test, and responds that he's never violated the law and eaten anything unclean (Acts 10:14).
- ***Given the purpose of these laws, what is God teaching Peter here, do you think?***
  See verse 28: that God no longer expects ethnic Israel to remain distinct from Gentiles, for his gospel is for the "unclean" as well as the "clean."

---

4. **Why was Peter's presence in Cornelius' house in itself a strange occurrence (v 27-28)?**
   Caesarea was the cultural meeting place for Romans and Jews. But they did not meet in each other's homes. Gentiles visited the homes of other Gentiles, and Jews did the same with other Jews. The Jews kept to themselves. No Jewish person would have set foot in Cornelius' house before.
   NOTE: Overestimating the distinction in the 1st-century Jewish mind between Jew and Gentile is almost impossible. The Jews despised the Gentiles. In the Jewish worldview, everyone was divided into Jews or Gentiles. If you were a Gentile, God neither loved nor chose you. He did not offer salvation to the Gentiles. Thus, what Peter says God has shown him (that he should call no person clean or unclean) presents a truly colossal shift in understanding.
5. **How did Peter connect his vision with his Spirit-given command to go and see Cornelius (v 28-29, 34-35)?**
   - v 28-29: No person is "unclean"—that is, Peter should not remain aloof and set apart from Gentiles simply because they are not Jews.

- v 34-35: "God shows no partiality." God does not favor the Jews simply because they are Jews: those who fear God and do what is right are accepted by him. And so the gospel is for Gentiles as well as Jews. Peter is not to offer the gospel only to those who are "clean" (Jews) but also to those who have previously been viewed as "unclean" (Gentiles).

6. **What does it mean to fear God and do what is right (v 35), according to verses 36-43?**
It means to be someone who "believes in [Jesus]" in order to receive "forgiveness of sins through his name" (v 43). Peter preaches the gospel of Jesus, the "Lord of all" (v 36). Peter's gospel proclamation to these Gentiles focuses on the same truths about the Lord as his proclamation to the Jews had done. There is one gospel, and those who fear God do what is right, which is to come to Jesus as Lord for forgiveness.

NOTE: Some believe Peter's words in verses 34-35 to mean that Cornelius was an "anonymous Christian." Anonymous Christians, according to this view, exist in every culture. They are people who do not know they are Christians. "Anonymous Christians" supposedly still worship the one true God, even if they've never heard of Christ. But this cannot be right. Jesus himself said, "I am the way, and the truth, and the life. No one comes to the Father except through me" (John 14:6); and the New Testament makes clear that salvation comes only to those who believe in Christ and repent of their sins (Acts 4:12). This episode itself shows that this view cannot be right: for if God had already redeemed and accepted Cornelius, he would not have needed Peter, nor the gospel Peter preached!

7. **How do verses 44-48 show that Peter was right—that the gospel was breaking through another barrier, to the Gentiles?**
God sent the Holy Spirit on Cornelius and other Gentiles who heard the word (v 44). Then these Gentiles began speaking in tongues (10:46). There is therefore, as Peter points out, no reason at all to withhold baptism, since the Lord has not withheld that of which baptism is a sign: salvation by faith and the gift of the Spirit (v 47). So, just as in Acts 2, these new converts to Christ are baptized (10:48). The coming of the Spirit on the Gentiles and their speaking in tongues is meant to remind us of Pentecost. It demonstrates that the same Spirit has fallen on both Jews and Gentiles, so they are one body—united by faith in Christ and members of his church. This was, in effect, Pentecost for the Gentiles.

8. **What did Peter need to understand and then do in order to be in a position to declare the gospel to these Gentiles?**
To understand that no one is outside the offer and reach of the gospel. This

required Peter to be willing to hear God speak and change his thinking appropriately; and it required Peter to be willing to do things he had never done before (such as visiting a Gentile's house) in obedience to God's word and the Spirit's prompting.

- **What are the lessons of this for you as individuals and as a church?**
  We need to be always willing to hear God speak to us in his word, and allow his Spirit to show us if we have something wrong. We are to be humble enough to have our minds changed by what God reveals in his word. And then we need to be obedient to what God tells us to do, even where that takes us outside our comfort zones, and calls us to do things we would not have expected or do not find easy.

9. **What is at stake—for us too, 2,000 years later—in verses 2-18?**
   The "circumcision party" understood that Jesus was the Messiah. But these Jewish Christians did not understand that salvation was not only for the Jews, who had waited hundreds of years with great expectancy, but was also for the Gentiles. If their view had been upheld and Peter's rejected, then the gospel would not have been offered by the church to those of us who are not Jewish. There would have been no great expansion of the church into Gentile lands through the rest of the book of Acts. There would be no church anywhere, including in Europe, North America, and Australasia (except as a small sect among Jewish populations). Much was at stake!

Explore More

- ***Before moving on, it is worth asking the question: how should Christians think about circumcision? Read Colossians 2:8-14. How does this passage help us?***
  We see here that the physical circumcision that God had commanded of Abraham and his physical descendants in Genesis 17 pointed to a true and better circumcision that is now a reality in the new covenant: circumcision of the heart. While circumcision under the old covenant was enacted with human hands, under the new covenant it is a spiritual matter; as Paul notes in verse 11, it is one that comes "by the circumcision of Christ." Just as bodily circumcision denoted a ritual cleanness and was a physical sign of separation from ungodly nations, circumcision of the heart denotes separation from sin and from the ungodliness of the world. A circumcised heart denotes devotion to God and to his ways.

10. **How do events in Antioch mirror Peter's visit to Caesarea, and extend what was happening there (v 19-26)?**
    The church had spread to areas like Antioch (north of Jerusalem) and Judea and Samaria (in modern-day

Syria) because of the persecution in Jerusalem (v 19), but the gospel was only proclaimed to Jews (v 19). Now Christ is preached to "the Hellenists"—Greek-speaking non-Jews. "A great number who believed turned to the Lord" (v 22), just as Cornelius' household had. As Peter and John had visited Samaria to see what God had done and celebrate it (8:14-17), so Barnabas and then Saul visit and minister in Antioch to see and celebrate what God has done among the Gentiles there. Here is the first majority-Gentile church.

11. **How does the church—now made up of Jewish and Gentile local churches—display its unity (v 27-30)?**
A prophet, Agabus, "stood up and foretold by the Spirit that there would be a great famine over all the world" (v 28). This famine likely occurred sometime between AD 45 and 47.

In response, the Antioch church determined "to send relief to the brothers living in Judea" (v 29). Verse 30 confirms that they carried through these intentions. This was a wonderful expression of unity. As we have just seen, the church in Antioch was predominately Gentile. The church in Jerusalem was Jewish. But both were Christian. And, as brothers and sisters, they supported one another. The Jerusalem church did not even need to ask the Antioch church for money; the Gentile Christians simply "determined" when they heard the prophecy of the famine that they should give money.

NOTE: While it may be striking to hear a group of people in the New Testament referred to as "prophets," we must remember that the gift of prophecy was still active during the time of the apostles (1 Corinthians 12:10). In fact, prophets will continue to appear throughout the book of Acts (Acts 13:1; 15:32; 21:9).

12. **To what extent are these qualities things that your church is known for?**
Where you are being challenged as a church, seek to foster positive discussion: if you are not known for one (or more) of these things, what would it take to change in this area so that you could be described in this manner? (Note that these three things are not the only qualities a local church might strive to be "known for" by other churches. But these are the three that are in sight here in this passage.)

- **How about you personally?**
Encourage your group to think about in what specific, practical ways they will seek to contribute to their church becoming known for the things the Antioch church was.

8

The Apostle, the Angel, and the King

Acts 12:1-25

The Big Idea

The plans and lives of the most powerful people in the world are under the control of our almighty God, who builds his church—so we watch for answers to our prayers and we live for his praise and not our own.

Summary

This section is filled with intrigue, politics, and drama. Luke's opening words, "about that time," shift the setting away from the previous scene at Antioch. But these words also signal a shift in the narrative. Luke is going to take his readers back in time to recount what happened to the church at Jerusalem.

The narrative centers on two men: (1) Herod Agrippa (grandson of Herod the Great, who sought to kill the infant Jesus), who was king by Roman permission but with Jewish blood and therefore attempted to position himself to the Jews as a loyal, devout Jew; and (2) the apostle Peter.

Herod had executed James, the brother of John (v 2). Since this pleased the Jews, he proceeded to arrest Peter (v 3). Herod no doubt wanted to execute him as well and continue to gain favor with the Jews. There was only one problem: it was during the days of Unleavened Bread—that is, the Passover. According to Jewish custom, no executions could occur during the Passover, so Herod had to wait. In the meantime, he put Peter in prison and ordered four squads of soldiers—16 guards in total—to keep watch.

The church did not despair; nor did it rise up in resistance. They prayed. And God provided an angel who told Peter to get dressed and then led Peter out of the cell. The church was so taken aback that Peter was free that they could not believe it—they had prayed faithfully, but had not believed fully that their prayer might be answered. We, too, need to learn not only to pray dependently, but to then be watchful for how our prayers are answered (Colossians 4:2).

Luke then switches the focus back to Herod, who interrogates and executes the unfortunate prison guards (Acts 12:19), and then moves "down from Judea to Caesarea." This is an important detail—Caesarea was the most "Roman" city in the region, so it indicates that Herod was giving up the ruse of being a good Jewish king.

But, as Luke recounts, Herod has little time to live. When the crowd in Caesarea ascribe divinity to him (v 21-22)—something the Jews would never have done, but which was a common reaction to royalty in the eastern half of the Roman Empire—he is struck down. His judgment, verse 23 explains, is because he stole glory from God, rather than giving it to God. Our pretense of being something more than we really are is ultimately the epitome of foolishness. Our ultimate end is to be worm food (v 23); only the God who made us, and who made the worms, is enduring and eternal. When we forget this, we lose our humility, and we lose our awe that God would be in any way mindful of us (Psalm 8:1-4).

The study finishes by noting that the Lord is more powerful than any human power, and will build his church despite any human opposition (Acts 12:24). Note how far the church has spread since the start of Acts, in just twelve chapters, as the Spirit works through the people of God to fulfill Christ's commission to his people in 1:8.

Optional Extra

To review your time in the book of Acts, and help jog your group's memories for questions 11 and 12, watch The Bible Project's illustrated video summary of Acts 1 – 12. Search for "Read Scripture: Acts Ch. 1-12" on YouTube.

Guidance for Questions

1. **Which person on earth has the most influence or power over your life?**
   Power manifests itself in different ways and can be used for good or ill—so in one sense a spouse has power over their spouse in terms of what their life is like (and, in this sense, even our children do!). But guide your group to think about their boss at work, or local elected officials, or the ruler of your country (be it a president, prime minister, etc). We may never meet these people, but they have the power to affect our bank balances, how we drive, and even our freedom. This question introduces Herod, who, as king of Judea, had huge power (albeit constrained by his Roman masters). Tell your group that we shall see in this study the different ways in which people responded to that power, and what it did to Herod himself.

2. **What new way did he now find to curry favor with the Jews (v 1-4)?**
   Herod killed James the brother of John with the sword. James and John were the sons of Zebedee, the "Sons of Thunder" (Mark 3:17). When Herod saw that the execution of James pleased the Jews, he proceeded to arrest Peter (Acts 12:3). Knowing Peter's influence in and over the fledgling church, Herod no doubt wanted to execute him as well and continue to gain favor with the Jews.

   There was only one problem: it was during the days of Unleavened Bread: that is, the Passover. According to Jewish custom, no executions could occur during the Passover, so Herod had to wait. In the meantime, he put Peter in prison and ordered four squads of soldiers—16 guards in total—to keep watch (v 4).

3. **How did the church react to Peter's imprisonment?**
   The church knew the sword waited for

Peter if God did not intervene. They knew what Herod had done to James, and knew he wanted to do the same to Peter. And so they prayed. They neither despaired nor sought to rely on themselves and rise up to fight back. They prayed.

- **How did God respond to Peter's imprisonment?**
  He sent an angel to remove Peter's chains and guide him out of the prison (v 7-10). Peter himself acknowledged that this rescue was the Lord's doing (v 11).

4. **Given that the Christians were praying for Peter's release, what is strange about their reaction to him standing on the doorstep in verses 13-16?**
   Rhoda, the servant girl at the door of the gate, evidently knew Peter well and recognized his voice (v 14). But instead of letting Peter in, she left him standing there and ran to tell those inside the house. Poor Peter was stuck outside, probably looking over his shoulder, wondering whether another divine rescue would be necessary.

   Still more strange, though, was the church's reaction. The very people who had been praying for Peter's rescue tell Rhoda she is out of her mind for telling them that their prayers have been answered (v 15). This suggests that they had no great expectation that their prayers would be answered in the manner they were asking for. They had seen answers to prayer before (e.g. 4:23-31), yet they clearly did not believe that they would see them now.

5. **Read Colossians 4:2. What does Paul tell us we should be when it comes to our prayers?**
   As we "continue steadfastly" in prayer, we are also to be "watchful in it" so that it might be with "thanksgiving." The paradox of praying faithfully but not really believing our prayers will be answered is one that afflicts us often, just as it did the church in Acts 12. We pray to the God "who is able to do far more abundantly than all that we ask or think" (Ephesians 3:20), so we would be wise not only to ask but to keep watch for answers beyond what we had hoped for.

- **How can you avoid the mistake of the Christians in Acts 12, and instead be "watchful"?**
  Simply by looking for answers to our prayers—either in the way we have asked, or beyond what we have asked, or in a different way than we have asked. If we ask God to help us with something in the morning, we should walk through our day looking out for how he is answering that.

- **How would being watchful both motivate and shape your prayers, do you think?**
  Prayers answered today drive us to our knees tomorrow. Often believers do not pray because they functionally believe that their prayers make no difference. As we watch for answers to

our prayers, we are able to reject that lie. We will also (as Paul says in Colossians 4:2) pray with "thanksgiving" more as we see our prayers being answered. Further, we will pray more boldly, for we will know that God is powerful and active in answering our prayers—even those (such as this one in Acts 12) that are asking him to do what is far beyond us.

6. **What do you think was the significance of Herod locating himself there, instead of in Jerusalem?**
   Caesarea epitomized Rome; it was the most Roman of all the cities. By moving there, Herod was giving up the ruse of being a good Jewish king. Josephus, the Jewish historian, argues that this was the moment Herod changed his persona and decided to become transparently Roman rather than seeking to pretend to be Jewish.

7. **What do Tyre and Sidon ask Herod for, and why (v 20)?**
   They ask for peace with Herod, and an end to his anger. They have befriended the influential Blastus, the king's chamberlain, in order to support their cause.

   The reason for such urgent pursuit of peace is that they depend on Herod's jurisdiction to provide them with food. Both were large commercial port cities lacking an agricultural sector. As a result, they depended on the irrigated land of Judea for food. They were, in a sense, at the mercy of Herod for provision.

8. **What was that response (v 22)?**
   They effectively began to worship Herod, shouting, "The voice of a god, and not of a man!" In other words, they were ascribing deity to Herod.

9. **What happened next, and why (v 23)?**
   - "An angel of the Lord struck him down."
   - "He was eaten by worms."
   - This happened as a result of God's judgment on him "because he did not give God the glory." Herod gladly received the praise of others without reference to God—and worse, he allowed others to treat him as a god without pointing them to the one true God. He stole God's place and God's glory.

- **How does the man who had escaped Herod's clutches show us the right response to receiving praise and honor? (See 3:12-16; 10:25-26.)**
  Peter was actually several times in a similar position to Herod here—being worshiped and praised as divine or semi-divine. But each time, he immediately rejected such praise, declared himself a mere man, and pointed people to God, encouraging them to praise him. Peter was always quick to point all praise and honor to the one who alone deserves it.

  NOTE: Some wonder whether God's pursuit of his own glory is self-absorbed and reveals some moral defect. Isn't self-promotion inherently wrong? Doesn't the Bible condemn seeking our own glory? Yes—but, these criticisms fail to understand that the Bible condemns men seeking their own glory, not God's. It is wrong for us to exalt ourselves, because we are mere creatures. But God is the eternal, infinite Creator and it is right for him to receive glory, and therefore to pursue his own glory.

Explore More

- ***Read Psalm 8. How does a right view of God, and of ourselves, cause us to live with...***
- ***right humility?***
  v 1-4: We are not the one who made everything. We are very, very small even compared to the works of his hands, let alone to him himself. He has majesty; we do not.
- ***great dignity?***
  God is mindful of us, and cares about us (v 4). Not only this but he has given us a privileged position (v 5) and rule over his earth (v 6-8). We are not God, but we have dignity as God's cared-for regents.
- ***Given the truths of this psalm, what would it look like to...***
- ***make too little of ourselves?***
  If we think of ourselves as mere matter, or no more valuable than animals, or unimportant to God, then we are failing to recognize the position God has graciously given us. We are more important to him, and have more inherent dignity, than grass or rabbits.
- ***make too much of ourselves?***
  If we think that we are the center of our world, and that we have the right to decide issues of morality or truth, then we are seeking to act as the Creator, and not as mere creatures.

10. **Herod was a powerful, influential king. What does the inclusion of Acts 12:24 remind us about human power and God's plans?**
    Luke records the growth of the church after Herod's death to contrast the wisdom and power of the world with the wisdom and power of God. Herod was a great king, arrayed in splendor, and he received the adoration of the people, but in the end he became food for worms. His glory and power were fleeting. The word of God, however, increased and multiplied. Luke's message is clear: the kingdom of man is frail and weak; the kingdom of God is eternal and unconquerable. God was in charge—not Herod—so his church continued to be built.
11. **This is the last session in this first study guide to Acts. Sum up in a couple of sentences the ways in which the church has been transformed in twelve chapters.**
    Here is my summary: At the beginning of the book, the church consisted of about 100 Christians gathered in a single city who had nothing more than a seemingly impossible mission and a commitment to pray for God's help. Now, empowered by God's

Spirit and armed with God's word, those Christians have multiplied into the thousands, have spread into Judea, Samaria, and beyond, and include unlikely converts, such as an Ethiopian eunuch, a one-time persecutor of the church, and a Gentile army officer.

12. **How have the first twelve chapters of Acts given you...**
    - **a greater awe of God?**
    - **an increased reliance on and joy in his indwelling Spirit?**
    - **a more committed attitude toward your church?**
    - **a greater confidence in evangelism?**

    Ask your group to write short answers for themselves, before sharing them with the group. Clearly, the Spirit will have worked differently in the different group members, so answers will vary. Make sure you encourage your group to read and think about the Getting Personal section following question 12 in the Study Guide (page 54), so that they think through how to turn what they have seen in Acts into practical changes in their lives.

Go Deeper with the Expository Guides to

Acts

by R. Albert Mohler, Jr

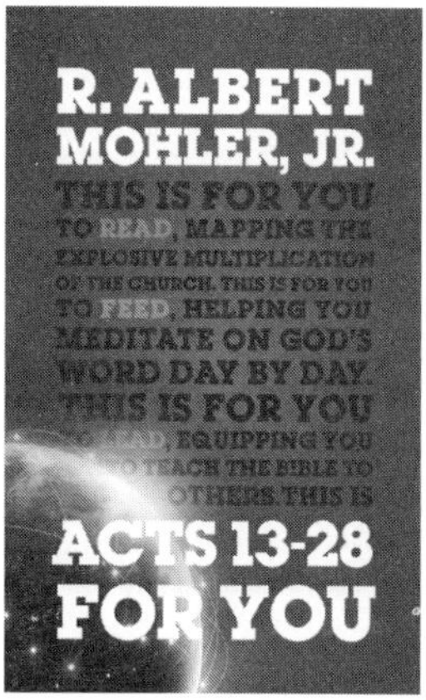

Less academic than a traditional commentary, these expository guides by Albert Mohler take you verse by verse through the book of Acts – thrilling your heart with this era-beginning, church-birthing part of Scripture.

This flexible resource can enrich your personal devotions, help you lead small-group studies, or aid your sermon preparations.

Explore the God's Word For You series

thegoodbook.com/for-you
thegoodbook.co.uk/for-you
thegoodbook.com.au/for-you